# Kerry Through its Writers

# Kerry Through its Writers

Edited by
Gabriel Fitzmaurice

NEW
ISLAND
BOOKS

**Dublin**

**Kerry Through Its Writers**

Is first published in 1993 by

**New Island Books**

2 Brookside

Dundrum Road

Dublin 14

Ireland

ISBN 1 874597 650

New Island Books receives financial assistance from
**The Arts Council (An Chomhairle Ealaíon)**,
Dublin, Ireland.

Cover painting by Pauline Bewick.
Cover design by Jon Berkeley.
Typesetting by Graphic Resources,
Printed in Ireland
by Colour Books Ltd., Baldoyle.

# Table of Contents

*I wish to dedicate this book to my friends, the writers D.J. Enright (England), Gyözö Ferencz (Hungary), Kazuo Ishiguro (England), Dedwydd Jones (Wales), Ed Leeflang (The Netherlands), George Szirtes (Hungary/England) and Liliana Ursu (Romania) who came and saw and imbibed the spirit of Kerry.*

# Introduction

It has become a commonplace to say that a given place is a state of mind. And yet, this is true of many places — of any place whose people re-create themselves in their environment. Kerry is such a place. We have been fed romantic, Celtic-twilight images of Kerry by the tourist industry with such success that not only do tourists flock to Kerry but that the natives half believe the soft-focus, tinted images of their lives.

What sort of place is Kerry? Look to the landscape — ocean, river, lake, mountain, hill, bog, pasture and plain. Some believe that a landscape explains a people, defines them. I don't know. But I *do* know that landscape influences people — who can not but be influenced by breakers in a gale charging the cliffs in Clochar or Ballybunion; who can not but be pared down to bare essentials by the mountains of Corca Dhuibhne or Uíbh Ráthach; who can not but be awed by a stippled sunset over Cnoc an Fhómhair or a silver moon tinselling a bog in Sliabh Luachra or Oidhreacht Uí Chonchubhair? Indeed. But what defines us is our language. We are what we can say.

Kerry has two languages, Gaeilge and English. The landscape is named in bastard English — a nonsense concocted from the original Irish by map makers for the Ordnance Survey in the nineteenth century. In their original form, the placenames "said" their landscape, translated it for its people. Kerry was *Ciarraighe*, "the territory of the people of Ciar," the son of Fergus Mac Roighe and Queen Maeve of Connacht. The name "Kerry" is, of itself, meaningless. Yet Kerry now means what it says: though lacking the historical and cultural resonances of *Ciarraighe*, it means today the place and its people.

Who are the Kerry people? John B. Keane has described the Kerryman as "the Greater, Hard-necked Atlantic Warbler... who quests individually and in flocks for all forms of diversion and is to be found high and low, winter and summer, wherever there is

7

the remotest prospect of drink, sex, confusion or commotion"! And that, indeed, is how many Kerry people are perceived. There is a larger-than-life, hyperbolic dimension to Kerry people. Cute and canny as they are, they seem to revel in living their lives in public — what other county has produced so many story tellers, singers, writers, footballers and talkers who *need* to perform in public. It is as if the closed, secretive atmosphere of the small village — and Kerry is full of small villages — explodes and displays all in public, like the person who won't confess privately to the priest, baring all to the nation on the radio.

I get the profound feeling that Kerry people need to express themselves, and will do so no matter what. And Kerry people like to hear about themselves. They flock to local "theatres" — parish halls, community centres — to see the latest John B. Keane play, curious to see themselves on stage. They make the required objections to the "vulgarity" of the language (knowing that vulgar means "of the common people" i.e. themselves) but are secretly delighted for they know that all is truth, that we are everything that happens, they see themselves reflected in the play. Kerry people, by and large, are big enough to take the rough with the smooth and are willing to see themselves as others see them. This is why, I think, they are so good at football. They are supremely confident in themselves, they know how to win and something deep down in them insists that they win in style. They know that all is truth on a football field and they play to create their own truth in the belief that the beautiful and the good will ultimately triumph. This is also, probably, why Kerry people are so loath to tolerate failure, especially in their footballers!

Kerry people are not parochial, unless one accepts Patrick Kavanagh's dictum that the parochial is positive, even universal, whereas the provincial is stifling and petty. Kerry people are inquisitive — "curious" is the way we say it here. They like to meet strangers, to find out about them, to talk to them. Many strangers, indeed, have put down roots among us and have become more Kerry than Kerry itself! In this book, visitors like Lily Van Oost, Mick MacConnell, Steve MacDonogh and Paddy

Bushe have gone native and live to tell the tale! Kerry people, I feel, welcome outsiders among them. They enjoy the exotic, the foreign, the fantastic and the fabulous. It must be remembered that we are now only one generation removed from being believers in the otherworld of the *sidhe*, the *piseog*, a magic world full of the possibility of good and evil. Scratch a Kerryman even today and you will find a superstitious streak. This streak is at once superstitious and religious. The vast majority of Kerry people still practise their religion — in most cases, the Roman Catholic faith, some Church of Ireland, and recently, some Jehovah's Witnesses who are making inroads in the heretofore conservative and traditional field of religious practice. Kerry Catholics, like most Irish Catholics, are partly pagan (and remember that "pagan" comes from the Latin "pagus" which means a village), and some of their traditional practices, patterns, holy wells etc., date back to pre-Christian Ireland. Unfortunately, the Protestant community is dwindling, many of their Churches closed and converted to arts centres, heritage centres etc.

Kerry people have traditionally lived off the land — farmers for the most, part-time fishermen, some-time labourers (anything to supplement the family income). The land varies in quality from rich arable land to poor, hungry land making life difficult for the subsistence farmer. It is no wonder, then, that Kerry has produced so many teachers, nuns, priests and brothers: that was the traditional way to improve one's station in life, though there is a well documented love of learning in the area as well. As early as 1672 Sir William Petty noted that "the French and Latin Tongues" were known "amongst the poorest Irish and chiefly in Kerry, most remote from Dublin!" On 27th May, 1673 the "Report of Lord Herbert, John Butler and Cadogan Barnes, Justices of the county of Kerry" commented that "the said County aboundeth...with youth learning of needless Latin instead of useful trades", and some twenty years later George Story, chaplain to Gower's regiment in the Williamite forces in Ireland, remarked that "every cow-boy amongst them (i.e. Kerry people) can speak Latin, on purpose to save them from the Gallows, when they come afterwards to be tried for Theft!" Indeed, until quite recently, Latin and Greek were compulsory subjects in colleges like Saint Brendan's in Killarney and Saint Michael's in Listowel. Living off the land kept people in tune with the cycle of the seasons. Even people who did not directly work on the land could not but be influenced by earth's diurnal course.

But all is truth, as I have said, and there is another side to the story. We have all read of cases like *The Kerry Babies* Brendan Kennelly's *Baby*, here included, was informed by this event); there is violence and crime (not as widespread as elsewhere, principally in cities, but nonetheless significant); and there is unemployment. Uíbh Ráthach (I prefer the original to "Iveragh" or "South Kerry") is severely disabled by unemployment and its consequent emigration. Other areas too. Parishes that could field a football team twenty years ago cannot now do so — unless father togs out with son to make up fifteen. *Something will have to be done* is the anthem of the unemployed. And soon, before it is too late and our most beautiful landscape becomes a playground or retirement home for the rich, the privileged, the foreigner and the speculator.

In compiling this book, I was interested to hear what native Kerrymen and women, and adopted Kerrymen and women, had to say. I was curious to hear how they would respond to Kerry. I left theme and tone open to the individual utterance — how it responded to life in Kerry, how it related to it, how it defined and was defined by it... The responses were various and vibrant. I learned more about Kerry, and ultimately about myself, from reading their contributions — no man is an island, and there is a sense that one is not simply of a county but that the county becomes one, that people are place and place is people. We have called up Kerry in language. Kerry exists in language, the song line of its people.

*Gabriel Fitzmaurice,*
*Applegarth,*
*Moyvane,*
*21st July 1993*

# The Kingdom of God and
# The Kingdom of Kerry

*John B. Keane*

Addressing the Old House of Parliament in Dublin in 1793, the great Irish advocate, John Philpot Curran, commented adversely that the magistracy of the county of Kerry were so opposed to the laws of the land that they were a law unto themselves, a Kingdom apart. The name stuck and at balls and banquets thereafter the Kingdom was toasted roundly as it is today after Kerry win the All-Ireland football final or a hard-fought golf tourney. In fact some Kerrymen say there are only two Kingdoms, the Kingdom of God and the Kingdom of Kerry.

Among other things this kingdom contains the next European parish to America which is Ballinaskelligs. Then there is Killarney of the lakes, Tralee of the Roses and Listowel of the Writers. The county contains a gossamer-like lunacy which is addictive but not damaging.

It contains dell and crag and mountain and a thousand vistas of unbelievable beauty. There is hardly a roadside where the ever changing chortling of a fishful stream cannot be heard. Then there is the towering, shattering, sometimes lagoon-like Atlantic which washes the shores of Kerry from Ballybunion to Kenmare. Ballybunion, beautiful beyond compare. What does one say about the champagne air and the daunting cliffs of Doon that has not already been said. Perhaps a tale from the past will serve better than an avalanche of laudatory adjectives from the present. Let us go back to the time of the Fianna, to the foot of Cnocanore.

Imagine Oisín, his father Fionn and a few more of the Fianna indulging in one of their less-favourite pursuits, i.e. assisting in the saving of hay for one of the local farmers. The meadow in question would lie near the cross of Lisselton which is about halfway between Listowel and Ballybunion. Overhead there is a clear sky and a balmy breeze blows inland from the nearby Atlantic. The time would be the latter end of June. There is a blessed silence all over the meadow with every man committed to the task in hand.

Then suddenly out of the distance comes the thunder of hooves. The Fianna, no less fond of diversion than any other voluntary labourers, lean on their wooden rakes and pikes and wait for the horse and, hopefully, rider to come within their ken. They have not long to wait for in less time than it takes to say rum and blackcurrant they are confronted by the comeliest of maidens astride a snorting white charger.

No cap or cloak, as the song says, does this maiden wear but her long flowing tresses of burnished gold cover the sensitive areas of her beautifully shaped body. Sitting erect on her steed she surveys the menfolk all around and a doughty bunch they are, each man more robust and more handsome than the next. No interest does she evince as her blue eyes drift from face to face. Then her gaze alights on Oisín, poet, philosopher, charmer and athlete.

She surveys him for a long times before she gives him the come hither. He hesitates.

"Come on" she says.

"Where? asks Oisín.

"Tír na nÓg" says she.

"Go on man" urge the Fianna in unison. No grudge do they bear him for such was the code of the Fianna. He hesitates no longer but throws his rake to one side and, with a mighty bound, lands himself behind her on the back of the magnificent white steed.

"Gup outa that" says she and the next thing you know they have disappeared altogether from view.

"Where did she say they were going?" old Fionn asks anxiously.

"Tír na nÓg" the others answered.

"It must be some land to the west of Ballybunion" the old chief surmises and without further ado he addresses himself to a swathe of hay.

The time went by and men and women went about their business. Then one day at that part of the Listowel-Ballybunion road known as Gortnaskeha the white horse reappeared bearing upon its back the handsome Oisín and the beautiful golden-haired woman. They came upon a number of men trying to move a large boulder from one side of the road to the other. All their efforts were in vain. They could not budge the boulder. Oisín leaned down from the horse and with his ludeen moved the great stone to one side but in so doing, poor chap, he fell forward on his face and eyes from his seat.

As he lay on the ground, exhausted and worn, the blonde spurred her horse and was never seen again in that part of the world although other blondes were to surface in Ballybunion with unfailing regularity year after year down to this very day and everyone of them as lovely as Niamh of the Golden Hair, which was the name of Oisín's partner.

Finding himself unable to rise Oisín placed a hand on the leaning shoulder of one of the Gortnaskeha men.

"I've been in Tír na nÓg" he said.

"Tír na nÓg" they exclaimed in wonder, for all had heard of it.

"Tír na nÓg my tail" said an old man with a dudeen in his mouth. "Ballybunion he's been to."

"But how did he age so much?"the others asked.

"Listen my friend" said the old man, "if you spent a weekend in Ballybunion with a blonde the like of what we saw on the white horse you'd have wrinkles too."

Which all goes to prove that a long weekend in Ballybunion can knock more out of a man than a score of years anywhere else.

Nearby is my native, beautiful Listowel, serenaded night and day by the gentle waters of the River Feale, Listowel where it is easier to write than not to write, where life is leisurely and beauty leads the field, where first love never dies and the tall streets hide the gentle loveliness, the heartbreak and the moods, great and small of all the gentel souls of a great and good community. Sweet, incomparable home town that shaped and made me!

Killarney is the gateway to the south-west of the Kingdom and so beauteous and captivating are the vistas thereafter that one is lost without a loving companion to share the pain and the hurt that great beauty induces. Without the love of my heart beside me I, personally, am lost here.

In 1842, at the age of 32, Tennyson wrote about this enchanted region:

*The splendour falls on castle walls,*
*And snowy summits old in story*
*The long light shakes across the lakes,*
*And the wild cataract leaps in glory.*

Yes. Tennyson knew and loved Kerry. Kerry, however, is as much its people as anything else. Once, years ago in my native town of Listowel, I listened to an overheated Redemptorist preacher as he ranted and raved about the declining morals of Kerry folk. On my way from church I asked an elderly friend what he thought of the sermon. Said he:

"His fulminations will have the same effect on the morals of Kerry people as the droppings of an underfed blackbird on the water levels of the Grand Coulee Dam."

The Kerry attitude to life is spiced with sarcasm and humour. There is a jaundiced undertone to all our observations and we have a fine contempt for pomp and vanity. Other counties joke about us but they must not be taken seriously for what is a critical county after all but an organisation that revels in its own imagined supremacy and, to cover its inadequacies, frequently makes up cheap jokes at the expense of its neighbours.

Long, dull sentences, especially religious and political, are anathema to the true Kerryman. The well-made, craftily-calefacted comment, the stinging riposte and the verbal arrows of cold truth will always penetrate the armour of cant and hypocrisy in the eyes of Kerry people.

We tend to digress as well but we do so for a purpose. Kerry folk know that there is no such thing as a truly straight furrow or a simple answer. Our digressions are what oases are to desert nomads, what incidental levities are to pressurised, underpaid workers, what the sideline fracas is to the bored onlooker. To a Kerryman life without digressions is like a thoroughfare without side streets.

I might write about other aspects of Kerry such as its fishing and its horse racing (over twenty days in all), or I might outline for you the course of a particularly well-taken score from boot to goal posts but I think it's more important that we concentrate on the living lingo of the Greater, Hard-necked Atlantical Warbler known as the Kerryman who quests individually and in flocks for all forms of diversion and is to be found high and low, winter and summer, wherever there is the remotest prospect of drink, sex, confusion or commotion.

He loves his pub and he loves his pint and he will tell you that the visitor, no matter where he hails from, is always at home in the Kingdom. He is hospitable to a fault but he eschews everyday language. I remember only last November to have been involved in an argument about the value of a trailer-load of peat for my winter fires. A countryman friend, in order to bring down the price, spoke disparagingly of the trailer's contents.

"A young blackbird" said he "would carry more in its beak."

Then there was the Kerryman in a Dublin hotel who was given fat rashers for his breakfast. Said he: "There wasn't as much lean in them as you'd draw with a solitary stroke of a red biro!"

There is no such entity, by the way, as a conventional Kerryman. If you try to analyse him he generates confusion. He will not be pinned down and you have as much chance of getting a straight answer from a cornered Kerryman as you have of getting a goose egg from an Arctic tern.

Your true Kerryman loves words, however, and that's a sure way to get him going. Snare him with well-chosen words and outrageous phrases and he will respond, especially if he's intoxicated, with sempiternal sentences, sonorous and even supernatural. On the other hand he has the capacity for long, perplexing silences.

It is when he is speechless, however, that he is at his most dangerous. He is weighing up the opposition, waiting for an opening, so that he can demoralise you.

One evening last summer as I sat outside a pub in the shadow of Beenatee Mountain in Caherciveen, the old Gaelic teacher with whom I had been drinking for most of the afternoon told me that the reason Kerrymen were so articulate was because the elements were their real mentors.

"They can patter like rain" said he, "roar like thunder, foam like the sea, sigh like the wind and on top of all that you'll never catch one of us boasting."

Kerry's two great peninsulas provide a topographic mix which no guide book, atlas nor survey map can adequately convey.

There are mountain lakes and waterfalls, mysterious inlets, sheer cliffs and golden beaches, breathtaking in their vastness, where frequently I have not encountered another human in the round of a summer's day.

The peninsulas of Kerry are only half-discovered. Everywhere along your route are tiny roads leading to secret slips and piers and periwinkle-studded rocks where the bright water laps and laves.

The flatlands of the Maharees on the Dingle peninsula boasts Fermoyle strand which is overshadowed by Mount Brandon, called after Brendan the Navigator, patron saint of Kerry and discoverer of America whatever the Spanish might say. These golden sands enchant the holiday-maker who seeks peace and solitude. Bring a bucket and a small rake and you will fill the bucket with luscious cockles inside an hour. Knock at any farmhouse in the vicinity and you can have them boiled, free of charge, with a mug of tea thrown in. They appreciate visitors here because the region needs them if only to take the bare look off the landscape.

Schools of dolphins traverse the adjacent seas and occasionally pause to stand on their tails on the water to execute their own Irish jigs when they spot humans on terra firma. If you wish you can make the acquaintance of Dingle's own resident dolphin, Fungi, by simply hiring a boat.

This is a landscape I know and love. Where else could I walk for an entire afternoon in my pelt in the certainty that I am safe from prying eyes. As a precaution I carry bathing togs on top of my head but am never called to use them.

The Ring of Kerry takes in the peninsula of Iveragh with its smaller peninsulas — dotted with quaint coves, rock pools and comfortable pubs that specialise in fresh seafood. From the windows of these amiable establishments one can watch the ebbing and flowing of the tides in comfort.

The towns of Kenmare, Caherciveen, Waterville and Sneem are all on the Ring of Kerry route and I stay sometimes at the Lansdowne Arms in Kenmare where the landlords will sing with me and their other customers in the blissful Kerry night.

Away from the golden sands are sallow-fringed streams, rivers and lakes where one can enjoy a preview of paradise. I have often escaped the turmoil of town and city to walk their calm banks, visited by so few.

I recall many such glorious occasions and one in particular, a little way from Dingle town with its fishing fleets and elegant streets, no two of which are alike.

It was that time of evening when light resigns itself to half light, yielding finally to darkness and it seemed that all nature was aware that stillness was needed if honourable surrender was to take place. In Kerry, with its magical retreats, one can experience such tranquillity.

There is an achingly beautiful road to drive between Kenmare and Sneem which takes you along the shore of Kenmare Bay past Templenoe and Parknasilla where Shaw wrote Saint Joan and earlier Gaelic poets were fêted.

This road continues on to Caherciveen and Waterville where lofty mountains gently slope down to the lap of the sea. On such journeys one never tires of driving. You will see no speeding cars on these winding roads and you may exercise your limbs on river, beach or mountain, or dawdle to your heart's content in absolute privacy. Whatever you wish to see by way of lake, river, rill, hill, mountain, sea or shore, is available, free of all charge, save for the verbal homage this area so richly deserves.

# The Sergeant

*Mary Cummins*

Past Lisselton, on the road between Ballybunion and Listowel, there is a spot in Ballydonoghue that divided my father's terri tory from that of Listowel. There is a pub, the Thatch of the Half Way House and a stream near it, that marks the line. He pointed it out once. My parish ends here, he said. A bit self-conscious he was, using the language of another power structure. But that was how he saw his jurisdiction. There were other markers on the roads to Tralee and Limerick.

He knew them. Inside those boundaries he knew every stick, stone and person. In those days, in the Fifties and Sixties, he would cycle to those boundary lines frequently. The Listowel road was straight but up Doon and on to Rahavannig or Beale, he would push his bicycle up the hills, mount at the top and cycle down the other side. The other guards would do it too, in turn.

When he did not cycle out the country, he went for a walk every afternoon in winter. In summer, if it was fine, he went down to the Long Strand every afternoon for a swim. Like everything, he did it according to the rules. Wading out until the water was up to his chest he would swim parallel with the shore or swim in. He never went into the water before the end of May. He taught us to swim, holding up your chin while you flailed around trying to get the guts to lift your feet off the sea-bed. In those days there was only one lifeguard. There was usually at least one drowning every summer. For a day or two a pall of quiet and grief would hang over the town even though they were usually visitors and you would not have known them.

You could set your watch by him every day when he went to the post office at about a minute to four. He would drop all the brown envelopes with the harp on them into the box and then set off down to the strand, walking in long strides, sometimes as far as the Cashen. This was his routine from after the Listowel Races

19

when Ballybunion closed down until the following Easter, if the weather was good, or Whit.

Walking back the Long Strand, he would take in deep breaths, sometimes stopping for a minute. On fine days, when you could see nothing except the glassy sea and the coast of Clare, the sea gulls swooping, he would say, "Isn't this grand. Think of all those people stuck in cities, working away in the heat and the smells. Look what they're missing," he would say, before striding off again. It has given me a life-long habit of fast walking, tireless until I stop and realise how far I've gone.

Before the sandhills skirting the golf course were eroded, there was an alternative route up and down the dunes, jumping over Kitty's River. If he was busy, he would only go as far as the 6th, mostly to the 9th and sometimes all the way to the 18th hole. Then, in the days of less bustle on the golf links, you could cross over to the Sandhill Road. That was before the new golf club was built. Long before the brand new clubhouse that replaced it this year, was thought of. The Taj Mahal, some call it.

Sometimes we would go into the graveyard at Kilahenny and examine the graves and look at the new headstones. Then back up to the Main Street. He would tip his cap to most people. "Hello, men," he would say to small groups at corners. One woman used to say, "Gooday sergeant. How's crime?" He got a kick out of that and would tell my mother when we got home. Sometimes, he would chuckle suddenly to himself — "How's crime".

On those afternoon walks he would wear a brown gaberdine coat (tweed sports jacket in summer) over his uniform. It was his usual attire unless we were going to Cork or Tralee or he was going to a family funeral. A few months ago, I saw a man coming towards me across the newsroom in *The Irish Times*. The face was familiar but it was his gaberdine coat over the blue shirt and navy tie that suddenly, after nearly 20 years, brought the image of my father back instantly. It was Lawrence Wren, the former commissioner. He had known my father and used to take Miss Carmody's house, next to the barracks with his family sometimes in the summer.

A few times a year, we would go on a really long walk up to the Hill (Cnoc an Áir where Fionn and the Fianna were supposed to have fought a bloody battle) and down the other side by Moohane to Ahafona and up by East End. Townlands merged into other townlands. After Rahavannig there was Derra, the dividing line from Ballylongford. Then Lahasreagh and Ballynoneen. He knew where each started and finished. He knew who was in every house, who had died there, who had emigrated and who had trouble or secrets. On a long walk out of the town, he might tell you things but not much. He was compulsively, obsessively secretive or discreet. Sometimes he would spell things backwards for my mother and we would try to guess. Sometimes they would talk in Irish. We would try to keep up.

This discretion passed on through the wives of the other guards. They had a special relationship. While they were part of the general life of the town, the ICA, doing the brasses in the church and suchlike, they were also particular friends with each other. Often, it was only the jobs of their spouses they had in common but that common, almost familial thing passed on to them, like a mantle of responsibility.

Then, the barracks was the centre of most business. Spring had arrived when the boards went up outside the door with notices on them to say it was a breach of a by-law to allow thistle, ragwort or dock grow on your land. The guards did the census and every thing else of an official nature so they knew everything. People had to come to get passports, for references, numerous other minutiae. There was little welfare. My father would send people — mostly women who were left widowed or abandoned — to Dan Spring in Tralee. Neither he nor my mother ever talked politics, but it seemed to be taken as read that it was Dan Spring who got things done. On 15th August, Pattern Day, Dan Spring's brother, Frank, who was the social welfare officer for the area, used our sitting room as the base for the annual ISPCC collection. There would be boxes everywhere and collectors coming and going.

There was no bank then in the town for much of that time. Some lending agency in Cork used to ring my father to find out about people's credit worthiness. If you hung over the railings on the landing at the top of the stairs you could hear bits of the conversation. You could hear my father telling the man what size the farm or the business was, if they were a good bet.

The lost children, who turned up kicking and hysterical every Sunday afternoon in the summer, were kept in the kitchen until their parents, red-faced, cross, relieved and sweating, arrived to claim them. People, usually men, being taken to the asylum in Killarney were kept in the sitting-room until they were ready to leave. Long after I left home, for me, Killarney still only meant the lunatic asylum. In the summer we often went to sleep to the howls and rich, roaring language of drunks in the "lock-up" which faced onto the backyard. They would bang the doors and curse and swear until they passed out, exhausted in the tiny cell.

On Sunday afternoons, my father and mother would go for a different walk. More of a stroll, usually up Doon Road and back by the Cliff Road. Stopping and talking to others. Sometimes they would meet the nuns and he would come back with accounts of how we were doing. My two sisters were hard-working and conscientious. I was bored and brazen, with a name for being clever. I got away with a lot. He used to say I was like his mother.

She lived in Cahirciveen where he was born. My grandfather, who was in the RIC, died young and left her with five sons. She reared and educated them on a tiny pension. She was supposed to be very strict and my cousin, Marian, who lived in Cahirciveen once told me that all the sons were terrified of her. I remember going to see her with my father. Once she gave me a ten-shilling note. I remember my father telling me that when he joined the guards he used to send her £2 a month. This was out of his pay packet of £8.

My father was from Kerry and my mother from west Cork. The Cork/Kerry thing only surfaced around the time of All-Irelands when they would banter about which team was best. But my father never openly showed a particular affiliation to Kerry. Maybe it was being in the guards. He had worked briefly in Dublin after leaving the Depot and hated it. He talked about having to walk in pairs on the streets around O'Connell Street and the open cheek they got from the Dubliners. Strict and authoritarian, he had no time for that and was disparaging about the natives of the capital. He had worked in a few different parts of the country but hardly ever referred to them.

We never argued, never talked back until after we had left home. From time to time he would say that Dev had been right not to get into the War. The country was too poor. I never knew if he was trying to rise me when he said the worst day for the country was when the English left. When I was drifting first into communism, and then into wet socialism, he would never argue but usually had some missile to throw me off my stride. He had no time for Conor Cruise O'Brien. Any man who would leave his wife... He did not spell it out but his strength of feeling was palpable. To him, to do such a thing was a total abnegation of responsibility. It spelt feckless, irresponsible, selfish. When I was raving on about Noel Browne one day, he corrected something and said yes, he had done such and such but it was when he was in Fianna Fáil. Noel Browne in Fianna Fáil? My youthful idealism was severely jolted.

He was never judgmental, at least in a language we could understand. He would describe someone as a blackguard. A rogue or a rascal was a lesser evil. Sometimes he used that description with humour in his voice. The only word of totally dismissive reproof that he used about anybody — usually a man — was, "he has no savvy". To this day I don't know what it means, but in the way he used it, no savvy meant that someone was not the thing. It was the ultimate dismissal.

His pride in the Garda Siochana, or the Force, as he usually referred to it was cosmic. There was no other body of men like it, no better members, no higher standards. There was a sort of universal pride thing in it that was almost familial. When someone got promoted, or someone else's children did well, it was almost as good as if one of us passed something. But also, if a guard broke a rule there was a muted sympathy in the air. There was no overt criticism. My mother used to talk sometimes about poor old this one or that one whom they knew from another place and who had a fondness for the drink or something.

One winter evening there was a knock at the door. It was a young man selling enclopaedias. He must have been badly off to come to Ballybunion off season. My father went out to talk to him and to our surprise brought him back and seated him up near the range and brought out a bottle of whiskey. Within minutes my mother was cooking a fry for him. It turned out that the young man's father was in the guards, somewhere up the country. They talked and talked and we ended up with a set of encyclopaedias that are in the house to this day.

He was a tidy, meticulous man with neat, small writing. Once he showed me one of the big books in the barracks in which every item was entered — when they came on duty, when they went off, what happened, when, where, how and why. He pointed to the glowing commendation written on it by the commissioner of the time. For the only time until he got sick our roles were suddenly reversed. He was looking for me, for my appreciation of what an important person had said about his work.

I only saw him as an ordinary person, subject to the rules of others once or twice. Once when very young, I was in hospital in Cork and was due to be discharged. Waiting all the night before into the dawn of the blessed day, I saw him suddenly walking down the polished wooden floor of the ward. A nun came hurrying after him, telling him he was not allowed in. She was stern, authoritative. I could not believe it when he looked abashed and retreated.

We got most of our good clothes in Tralee and we went there before Christmas. My parents knew the men who worked in the big shops, the Munster Warehouse, Lyons's and Revington's. They greeted them like old friends. And sometimes we would meet them when they were in Ballybunion during the summer. Getting coats and shoes or material was a leisurely affair. They would sit down and we would parade in a variety of colours and shapes until the right one was found.

We went to Cork for things not available in Listowel and Tralee. Every so often my father and mother went to have their eyes tested and their glasses changed. They had different doctors, both on Patrick's Hill. We always got a Fuller's cake to bring home. Once, on a trip there, I saw my father angry. We must have been parked in the wrong place. It was late in the evening of a long day. A young guard came up to the car window and started talking to my father who was in civvies. "And I suppose you want my name too?" my father said, while we all held our breaths. The young guard nodded, a bit less sure of himself. "Well, you won't get it", my father snapped. The guard backed off and my father drove off with us whooping with delight in the back.

That was when we were in Knocknagoshel because my father said we did not need the car when we moved to Ballybunion where there were many more services. Until then we had one of the old, high, black Ford's. It had a step down from the door and for much of the time sat in the haggard near the barracks. My father was a slow, tense driver. Going over the Healy Pass with its corkscrew twists and turns on the way to Adrigole, my mother would get her rosary beads out.

Now, when I hear people talking about the Office of Public Works, I remember the special wrath with which my father used to talk about them. They would only paint the outside of the barracks every eight years. I only remember the inside being painted once or twice. He had a life-long running battle with them to get them to change their rules. Once, he got a terrific kick out of putting one over on them. There were installing a newer range than the old black Stanley in the kitchen. I heard my father telling my mother how it was a special type that could eventually be converted so that radiators could be run off it. However, the OPW men were not aware of it.

The paraphernalia of coming from a garda family littered my childhood. Even though we only moved twice, to Knocknagoshel from Castletownshend and then to Ballybunion, the memory of changing house, school, friends, neighbours is vivid. So strong are the memories it seems we moved every year. It seemed as if the discussions about Nat Ross, what would fit and what wouldn't, what would be taken in the car or left behind, dominated much more than two postings. The first night in the new barracks was always full of excitement, so strong it was impossible to sleep. No proper beds, just mattresses on the floor. Drinking tea out of cups without saucers or plates. Rooting through orange boxes and tea chests where everything was anonymously wrapped up in newspaper.

In Knocknagoshel, the O'Conoers were all called "The Masters". There was Mrs The Master, Patsy The Master, Rory the Master and so on. It was years before I discovered that we were also similarly described: Mary The Sergeant, Mrs The Sergeant, Kathleen The Sergeant.

When my father said we were moving to Ballybunion, it was almost impossible to take in. I can only remember desperate, piercing happiness. For us Ballybunion was the most rapturous place. The sun always shone. We always had picnics. There was ice-cream. There were swings, roundabouts, travelling players who stayed for the summer. It surged with energy and bustle. The big hotels were the most exotic and untouchable things on earth. The sea was there, always. We ran out and told everybody and everybody was static with jealousy.

I must have been small. I remember Sister Aidan in the primary school taking me into my older sister's class because I was crying. I remember being cushioned in against her and only came up to her waist. I remember Joan Henderson, whose father was the most senior guard in the station, calling to take me back to school after lunch. We had a big tin of Kimberley biscuits — the really tall ones they had in shops which we had got as a present leaving Knocknagoshel. My father asked her some trivial question, like why did she like school or something. "Nowhy," she answered pertly, the two words used as one. I was dumbfounded. The sureness, the confidence of it, the sophisticated slang compared to Knocknagoshel where such smartness was unknown.

The barracks in Ballybunion was much bigger — not more rooms, just bigger, with a long landing upstairs and wide window-seats everywhere. You could sit there to read, hiding behind the curtains. We had no inside bathroom for a couple of years. Then, a small bedroom was turned into one. That has left me with an abiding yearning for bathrooms that are real rooms and big, cold bedrooms.

My father never drank much and hardly ever socialised in the pubs or hotels in Ballybunion. But as we got older, we would go into Mary O' Hanlon's through the back entrance and sit in the snug while he had a pint and I would have a glass of Harp. On rare occasions we would go to the Central Hotel for a drink. Whiskey or brandy was poured out liberally at home for visitors or relations. The shelves in the pantry off the kitchen were always laden with bottles of spirits. They arrived every Christmas from most of the pubs and hotels and were put away. I often wondered why they bothered since he still raided all the pubs and hotels anyway, winter and summer.

He was famous for being strict. Many stories, many of them apocryphal, were told about the degree of his strictness. Brendan Kennelly, who used to come to the dances in Ballybunion, said they always had to give the sergeant's daughters a duty dance in case they were caught without a light on their bikes going home. When I started work in *The Irish Times*, Jack Fagan told me how my father had run his brother out of town. The brother was tearing down the main street on a horse.

Babe Walsh who is married to Eddie Walsh, the famous foot-baller in Knocknagoshel, who went to live there around the time we were leaving, told me about a year ago that her husband always said my father was strict but fair. They have a pub.

He was never off-duty. If the barracks was closed people just came round to our door. The phone was always turned over to the living quarters, as they were called, if there was no-one on duty. Sometimes women rang in the early hours of the morning asking why he was not raiding such and such a place. They never gave their names. He never took holidays except to visit relatives. Years after he died, my cousin Liam who lived in Galway told me that he came to them every September. He was as regular as the swallows, Liam said. My Uncle Paddy, their father, died when they were still young. My father would visit them, just for a day or two. He would talk to my Auntie Maura and ask them how they were getting on at school, what they were going to do, how they did in exams. And then he would leave again.

One summer towards the end of his working life, he and my mother went around the Ring of Kerry on a coach tour. They talked about it for a long time afterwards. He smoked Gold Flake. He would send us across to Michael Beasley's for ten. One Lent he and the doctor gave them up and he stayed off them. Years later I asked him why he had given them up and he said to save money for us.

Even though he was on a low salary until his final years, we were never conscious of the need for money. We got summer jobs but unlike in some houses where the money was necessary, we never had to hand up our pay. We would buy our school books with it and a special outfit as we got older. I knew we were not rich. Not in anything like the league of the summer visitors, the doctor or the few prosperous publicans. There were no luxuries but there was no question of stinting for necessities. His money-management passed on to every other person in the family except me.

Probably the one addiction in his life was the pictures. In Ballybunion, there were three changes a week, Monday, Wednesday and Friday. He went to them all, unless work intervened. We were allowed to the matinee on a Sunday afternoon which was usually a Western, with no women in them. He sat around one of the two corners at either side of the entrance. We called it the old men's corner. Mr Johnny Lynch (hardware, undertakers, men's clothes), Mr J. D. (O'Mahony) (Imperial Hotel and famous publican), Jerry Breen (jeweller and watch-mender) and Doctor Hannon were some of the regulars. The opposite corner was called the courting corner. Unless you were near-engaged, you were considered fast if you went round there as of right.

Anything new fascinated and absorbed him, lifting his spirits for days on end. Once when we brought my sister to Dublin

Airport to get a plane for England, he watched every iota of movement and detail with avid eyes. When we got back to Dan Shanahan's car, he described every move from the minute we had left. Who had taken her luggage, what they did, what they looked like, but more especially the movements of the plane from when it started to rev up until it was in the sky. It moved forward, so, he said, describing the distance and the direction. Then it turned and stopped. Then, and then and then, until it was just a speck in the sky.

Dan Shanahan was the local hackney driver. He took us everywhere at a nice steady pace. I once heard my father describe him to someone as being as near to the perfect car driver as dammit. If everyone drove like Dan Shanahan, he said...

One summer evening, a man nearly drowned. He was a travelling salesman who had arrived late in town on a hot day. He decided to go for a swim about 8p.m. when the strand was almost empty. He was spotted and rescued by Ray Bailey, who was the life-guard for several years. Later he told my father how he struggled and then was certain he was going to go under. His life flashed before his eyes. He thought of his family and blessed the day he had taken out life insurance. My father told these kind of stories in such economic detail they always stayed in your mind. There is no history of writing on either side of the family but I have often thought that if I got a curiosity about people, a passion for stories and an obsession with straight facts and detail, it was from him.

Apart from putting either ha'pennies or farthings on the Railway line in Cahirciveen so that the train would flatten them out to the size of a penny and they could fool the poor-sighted woman in the local sweet shop, my father talked little about his own childhood. Another admission was that he had started smoking at fourteen, as I did. It must have given him a special sympathy when he found out, by chance, that I was at it at a young age. One day when we got soaked coming from school our raincoats were hanging up near the fire. He tried the pockets to see if they were drying out and found a pile of butts at the bottom of mine."You shouldn't be at that," he said. "They're bad for you."

But there was no special stricture, no lectures. Only, often after that, he would pass me stories about the horrors of smoking in the *Reader's Digest.*

He never did anything around the house, not even handy jobs. I don't think he was handy in that way. Also, I can never remember people putting up shelves in the way they now do or reconverting rooms. But every Sunday morning, when my mother went to first Mass, he cooked the fry. There would be newspapers spread within a wide radius of the range. There were plates stacked neatly. Everything was done in rotation, rashers first, then sausages and then the eggs. It was always perfectly timed.

Sometimes we would go down to Cahirciveen to stay with my aunt and uncle and visit relations. We would spend afternoons and long nights in Ballinaskelligs and Portmagee while the adults talked about this and that, this one and that one. Sometimes they dropped their voices and you couldn't hear what they were saying. Sometimes my mother would take some of us on to west Cork and leave one of us with my father. He was happy there. His voice and face lightened and he talked and laughed easily. Sometimes they would sit up late playing cards. He loved cards. He would go to whist drives in Ballybunion and sometimes in Listowel but the card-playing around Cahirciveen went on long into the night with roars of laughing every now and again. I could watch him for hours so different was he in that setting. I was quiet and they wouldn't notice me curled up in a corner, half-reading a book.

He kept a neat vegetable garden out in the back yard and grew tomatoes that trailed up the wall. They never ripened and were always brought inside, wrapped in newspaper and stored in cardboard boxes to ripen. He grew rows of lettuce, cabbage, potatoes, carrots and onions.

There was a big old trunk in the pantry. It had a special key and if you could find it you could delve into the trunk and roam through reams of papers like birth certificates, old photographs, old letters. I was very uncurious. Finding the key was more important than examining the contents.

His uniform was always spick and span. He polished his shoes himself until you could see yourself in them. It passed on. I can't bear scuffed shoes or heels that need repairing. Every Monday morning they had a special drill in the day room in the barracks at nine sharp. On that morning his silver buttons would be Silvo-ed and my mother would brush down the back of his jacket. He had a special, flat gadget that fitted around the buttons so that the liquid would not get on the material of his uniform.

He had a great regard for scholarship. He did not read much except the daily paper. They had to change from *The Cork Examiner* when we moved to Kerry. We had the usual collection of Canon Sheehan's, a few Brinsley McNamara's, the collected works of Shakespeare, James Stephens' *Crock of Gold* and some others. He used to say that if a person read the daily paper they would be educated and literate. When I got a job with *The Irish Times* he was very pleased. But, he said, in a moment of confidence, wouldn't it have been marvellous if it was *The Independent*. He cut out every piece I wrote and put them over the dresser. They were brought down for every visitor to the house. He looked over their shoulders while they read them. My friends would tell me this later, in fury more than in fun.

When television came in, he switched his loyalty from the cinema. He had a high stand made for the far side of the kitchen and the large television set stood in glorious, isolated splendour. He watched it all the time but made little comment except to say that at least Ireland could hold its own with everybody else now. He loved police things like *Hawaii Five-O*.

When this series had been running for some time he told me a story about how it was adding to his skills. He got intense delight in his cleverness in using the slick skills of the up beat, brainy young cops in Hawaii to crack a local crime. A young man had broken into a house for reasons too complicated to go into and did some damage. When the guards were called, there was precious little evidence except a vase that was found in a nearby field. My father was sure he knew the young man who did it — a fellow he liked. Neither did he disagree with his hot-headedness in this case. However, he had to know and the fella was playing dumb. One day my father called him into the barracks. They talked of this and that. Eventually the conversation came round to the break-in. Lowering his voice, my father looked towards a cupboard and said he had evidence that would prove who had done the damage. Carefully, with all the right dramatic moves, he used two handkerchiefs to lift the vase from the shelf. It was going to be sent "to forensic", he said, *á la* Jack Lord. When they got the fingerprints back the case would be all wrapped up. It was too much for the young lad who confessed on the spot.

He never spoke about happiness or unhappiness, about the meaning of life or death unless in the context of the drowning man. He liked going out occasionally. Even when he had to go to court in Listowel he would come back and give a blow-by-blow account of the dinner they had in the Listowel Arms. He liked good quality material and believed in paying a bit extra for quality.

The only place he ever said he wanted to visit was the Holy Land. He did not seem particularly religious or, at least, did not express his feelings. He was strictly moral in the sense of good and bad and did not spare his views on those who were either blackguards or were just conmen. He was probably the hardest person in the world to lie to. You felt he could see right through you, into your soul. I can't imagine anyone looking him straight in the eye and expecting to get away with a tall story. He did not suffer fools.

He died shortly after retiring when he was sixty-three. That was on 5th February, 1975. At the time it seemed old but now when I visit Kilahenny and see the other dates and ages on graves, I realise he was young.

That was my father. The sergeant. I am the sergeant's daughter.

(From *A Time for Voices*, Bloodaxe 1990)

# Baby

*Brendan Kennelly*

I find it interesting to be dead.
I drift out here, released, looking down
At men and women passing judgement
In the streets of that moneymad little town.
I enjoy the jokes about me, scribbled in the gents,
I like the lads in suits, their smart legal faces,
I follow them through every argument,
I note their gas antics at the Listowel Races.
There was a hope of love at the back of it all
And in spite of clever men making money
That small hope still survives.
Will I name the clever men for you? Yerra, no.
I smile to watch them prospering to their ends
But thanks be to Jesus I won't have to live their lives.

They're trying to find out who killed me,
A fascinating exercise.
If I were water I'd let them spill me
And I'd run out of their eyes.
If I were fire I'd burn books of law
And half-burn the men who study them.
If I were air I'd slip into their lungs
And out of pity revive them.
If I were earth — O now that I think of it
That's what I am or am becoming
A little more quickly than you, and painlessly.
Tell me what you think it means to be alive,
I'd love you on that topic, expounding.
Being dead, I must find out, you see.
And yet, being dead, I may grow

To be a small, cheeky flower
Peeping through a veil of snow
On the scarred face of the earth
That never grows ashamed;
Or I may be
A blade of grass to nourish you;
Or a book
Wherin the nosey world may read
Of lovers' luck
And what it means to bleed.

When I was being formed in her body
I could tell she was kind.
My toes my fingers my eyes
My hands my bum my tiny mind
Knew that.
She carried me everywhere.
I couldn't see where I was going.
She did.

Streets, roads, fields, kitchens,
Bedrooms, chapels, small hotels, fish and chips places,
Glances of men in cars, glances
Of women both barren and fulfilled —
I'm buried now under the strong feet
Of money. I'm dead. I hope my mother
Sings and dances.

# The Poet as Blow-In

*Paddy Bushe*

I'm a blow-in from Dublin. I've lived in Kerry for twenty years, almost half of my life. As a child I spent holidays in various parts of Kerry. This is my triple perspective on living in Kerry, a perspective whose aspects are constantly commenting, in various tones, on one another.

Let me give an example. On the Glencar side of Bealach Oisín there is a small bridge with one arched and one square opening. Passing it shortly after moving to Waterville, I was startled by an intense flashback of my father stopping the car there and all of the family tumbling out to watch him vainly "wet a line". I stood at this reclaimed spot as a father, a newcomer identifying landmarks, tentatively trying to send down roots, an outsider in love with a landscape. Nowadays when I pass that bridge, I curse the potholes, the meeting that involves a hundred miles round trip and many of the other things that come with the actual business of living. But the bridge is equally and continually in focus from any of the three perspectives. I am not foolish enough to think that only urban blow-ins with childhood memories can see a place from different points of view but I believe that the separateness of my perspectives allows me to eavesdrop with more understanding on their conversations.

Being a blow-in poet makes me part of a long established tradition going back to where Robert Graves claimed "English poetic education should begin". As I write, I'm looking out over Ballinskelligs Bay. It was here, we are told, that Clanna Mhíleadh, the first Celtic invaders set foot in Ireland. And here Amergin, a son of Milesius, recited his famous incantatory poem in which he identifies with the landscape, animal life and the very life force itself.

Mé gaeth ar muir
Mé seig i n-aill ...

This is the poem to which Graves ascribed such importance. Graves possibly never that knew his grandfather consecrated the small church which still shoulders off the Atlantic gales just above where Amergin landed, but somehow a circle seems completed. A version of the myth written by Sean Ó Conaill, a Kerry poet, in the 17th century has it that Éanna, a son of Milesius, was drowned off a rock in Ballinskellings Bay. Carraig Éanna lies just out from my house and gave me a name for my own son. Another circle completed. The story resounds throughout the landscape. Other sons of Milesius were drowned on Sceilg and the Bull Rock. Nearby standing stones and a dolmen are the reputed graves of warriors' wives. It is perhaps because I was a blow-in writer that the discovery of this mythological blow-in-writer and the attendant echoes attracted me so much and gave me a title for my first collection, "Poems with Amergin".

Of course I didn't blow in to just a literary landscape. There were bogs and meadows which I learned involved physical realities which were achingly and sweatily removed from the visual pleasure experienced from a passing car. Neighbours and friends, justifiably dubious about what help I would be, nonetheless welcomed me as apprentice (not that I'd claim to have earned my papers!) And there are poems in this too. My wife still recalls my coming home from the pub soon after we had moved in, and announcing that we would have to buy a freezer. "Why?" she asked sleepily. She was a little startled by my reply. "Because I met a man tonight and we bought a pig together." It was this sort of discovery, of sharing something new, that prompted the following poem when a great and good friend died last year.

GOING SHARES

(in memory of Denny Sugrue)


We went shares in a pig the first time
we drank a pint together, you ensconced,
me a tentative stranger in this place.
The years since saw many sharings,

nights of porter and stories not to be repeated.
In sweating bogs and meadows we shared days
when the work and the crack were endless
as your share of days appeared to be.

Your last draw was a short one, the whole lot
out and banked before we knew it.
I can see you now, high on the trailer:
*that's one noble load* of turf, you're boasting,

while with due ceremony, your face alive
with laughing, you clamp the final sod.

In 1973 I came to Waterville as a teacher. Later, when it was
safe to tell me, I found out that it was assumed locally that I
would be a disaster, since I obviously couldn't get a job anywhere
nearer Dublin! But teaching is a wonderful way of being introduced to a community. Families, townlands, rivalries, relation-
ships — students and their parents are an enormous data bank
waiting to be delved into. Mind you, there were some initial
lapses in communication, as when I expressed surprise to a first
year essayist who had "carried the sheep up the mountain". I
gained a new insight into the relationship between cartography
and the South Kerry landscape when I asked a student what he
thought the varying shades of brown on a 1/2-inch ordnance
survey map indicated. "The darker the brown, sir," he ventured,
"the deeper the slough."

Teaching, especially in a small community, is a socially enriching experience, and it introduced me to many facets of life in my
adopted area. Education is essentially an exploratory activity
both in the classroom and in the planning and administrative
area. During my teaching years I was involved in classroom,
administrative and trade union activities. Apart from inevitable
encounters with the odd — very odd — individual who viewed
educational decisions from either a paranoid or self-seeking
perspective, the whole process enhanced my understanding of life

in Kerry. And my understanding had to make sudden jumps. Faced with teaching History and Geography, and not having opened a book on either since my Inter. Cert., I had to engage in some hasty research in order to maintain a dignified bluff. Much of this crammed research was a revelation. Mountains, which had been a distant pleasure, opened into arrêtes and glaciated valleys, into moraines and corries and hanging valleys. Their stratified and folded sandstone layered itself into my mind. This intellectual exploration naturally led to physical exploration, and walking amidst the high and hidden places of South Kerry has been, for my wife and myself, one of the great joys of living in South Kerry. The sense of awe and wonder which this hillwalking aroused led to this poem.

### UIBH RATHACH MOUNTAINS

The old people, perhaps, knew them in a way;
driving cattle through the stony half-light
and early exhalations of a mountain path,
from Cúm a'Bhóthair to a fair in Sneem.

But in the making, before the dreamtime?
No strain of sweetness then. Deadness
settling, dust, sand and shells, sea-pressed,
growing taut, ignorant of the fire beneath the skin.

Until the molten throb, insistent as a drumbeat,
thrust hot. Then skin felt fire's course, clenched,
and buckled. Afterwards, the slow swelling.
Sediment grown prodigious bulged towards the sun,

but was clamped, under a sterile sheet
was probed with sharp steel, rang barren.
The swollen womb was scraped to cúm and cumar
still resonant of icy instruments.

Now larks and heather tell of gentler births.
At Eisc na Mactíre, Cathair na Gaoithe and Cúm Cathcon,
watchers smile at contoured map and compass;
Old faces at a wedding, their thoughts womb-deep.

Locality and landscape can also give an immediacy to history. Visits to Dún an Óir and its cliffs vivified the story of the infamous massacre of 1580 and the irony of two Elizabethan courtier poets — Raleigh and Spenser — being intimately involved in it led to a series of poems called "Poets at Smerwick". The echoes of Daniel O'Connell around South Kerry, especially in Derrynane, led me to write a series of poems called "Counsellor". In general the focus of the series is anecdotal and local rather than sweepingly historical. A sample:

*BOG*

*Scum condensed of Irish bog!*
thundered *The Times* from London
at O'Connell. All over Ireland
bogs continued their slow assimilation
of leaf, branch and root. Small pools
winked ambiguously in the sunlight
while heather nodded wisely in the wind.

In Derrynane Dan smiled and spread
his hands towards the turf fire.

I believe that poetry is enriched by a dialogue between past and present, especially when both past and present can be simultaneously discerned in a particular setting. The following poem, written during the debate on the Maastricht referendum, will serve to illustrate.

## COASTGUARD FORT

The cornerstones are huge
still framing a structure
toppled into ruin,
an allegory of empire

repeated around the coast.
These forts and towers once
beaconed nervous signals
from headland to headland,

empire in dread of empire,
while peasants below passed news
*concerning young Napoleon
and his bonny bunch of roses-o.*

Stone stairs mount ponderously
to where a homesick officer
his telescope scanning the sea
cursed the blasted heather,

the wind, his restless men,
the whispering peasants and Napoleon,
while his memory focussed
sharply on the home counties.

He might have laughed
if his telescope had seen
England, France, the bloody lot
congealed in a new empire,

the headland almost cleared
of peasants and their cabins
and they their own masters,
going begging to Brussels.

Lest, however, I overwhelm the reader with landscape and poetry, let me recall some more of the culture shocks that accompanied my moving to South Kerry. There was the man who seeing my wife with our weeks-old child insisted to her at great length (about me) that she should "get that shagger to marry you!" Another man, puzzled by the unusual name, and mindful of my then luxuriant hair and beard, was curious to know whether our real name was Shea or Sullivan. And my invincible ignorance about sport was no help when, on being told the name of the proprietor of the establishment where I was having a pint, I asked "who's Mick O'Dwyer?" A similar reaction greeted a similar question when I was told that Eoin Liston was to be our new Science teacher. It was a reaction something like I imagine a Martian visiting the Vatican would encounter if he were to ask after the Pope's wife. But nowadays, at least, my fervently believing son is there to counter his heretical father's blasphemies, and to celebrate or mourn after the Munster Final.

My most recent writing has been inspired by visits to archaeological sites in my own area. Of all of them, or of any of the places I imaginatively inhabit, it is Sceilg Mhichíl which draws me most. I have visited it numerous times, in varying weathers. Its pinnacles have transfixed my imagination and its birds and seals haunt my inner eyes and ears. Its physical and spiritual uniqueness place it beyond all places and yet there it is, behind that headland, eight miles offshore from where I write. I will finish with the words I attribute to the hermit who built the high, isolated cell on its almost inaccessible South Peak.

I will cling to this hard rock
until I become no more
and no less than a syllable
in the breath of the Word.

# Kerry

*Mick MacConnell.*

A young man dressed in blue jeans and a leather jacket was setting up keyboards, amplifiers and microphones on a stage at the end of the bar. We sat as far away as possible. I braved the Saturday night crowd of Listowel drinkers while Peter engaged in the preliminary ritual of charging his pipe.

By the time I got back with two pints, the pipe was drawing well. Wreaths of Mick McQuaid indicated that Peter was settling into his customary mode of relaxation. We studied the pints in silence while waiting for them to settle.

Peter spoke first. "Did you know that the man who wrote the song *"The Boys of Wexford"* is buried just a few miles out the road on the way to Tralee?" he asked .

I admitted that I didn't.

"I don't know much about him, in fact I don't even know his name, but he is buried there alright," Peter continued.

"He was probably in the same sort of boat as yourself. He must have wandered into Kerry and never managed to get out of it. Somebody told me that there is a plaque of some sort on his gravestone, but I never saw it myself. Maybe we might take a wander out there some day and see for ourselves."

We sat in companionable silence. I racked my brain for even a scrap of remembered knowledge about the man who wrote *"The Boys of Wexford"*! Nothing surfaced. And I wondered if the forgotten songsmith and myself had anything more in common than failing to escape from the lure of the Kerry Kingdom.

It was a comforting feeling that another man who grappled with the secret joinery of music-making had made the same pilgrimage long before me. I resolved there and then that I would make it my business to learn something about him.

"Testing! One! Two! Three! Four! ", boomed the young man from the stage.

Peter grimaced in distaste.

"God be with the days when you could walk down the streets of this town on a Saturday night and have your pick of the best music between Sliabh Luachra and Clare", he lamented. "Where has it all gone? It's a sorry pass when a man has to put up with this."

I offered no comment because the young man being castigated was a friend of mine and I knew for fact, was playing music with the sole aim of paying his mortage and feeding his wife and young family.

But Peter was off in full spate.

"There is damn all good music around nowadays. You wouldn't remember any of it. It has no lasting power. It says nothing and is played by incompetents for fools." He paused in recollection and then continued: "You know that some of the sweetest music I ever heard was played for free for the youngsters of the town by a couple of blow-ins like yourself. It was long ago now, but I can still hear it. He was a fiddle player and she played the piano. Freddie and Gertie they were called and they had a jewellers shop in the small square. Every Sunday in summer they would throw the windows open and play together in their front room. I was a lot younger then, but I still remember gathering on the pavement outside the shop. Every time they finished we would call out for another tune. I can still remember standing there as darkness fell with the sound of the fiddle and the piano washing around the blackening streets."

He was on his feet on his way to buy another round. Whereas my trip to the bar was a simple act of commerce, Peter's was more of a stately procession with stops every now and then to exchange a few words of greeting with friends and acquaintances.

He was one of the first friends I had made since moving to Kerry. He had taken me under his wing and had explained some of the secrets that Kerry people are born into. It was he who had given me the first glimpse of the key that unlocks the Kerry language and humour.

It was he who had explained that most towns in Kerry could be compared to tinker women who hang around crossroads with a few geegaws of trade in the hope of attracting unwary passers-by. All towns, he claimed, had their own distinct traits and personalities and should all be regarded with the same suspicion as tinker women.

By that reckoning, Listowel, the town I had chosen to settle in could be compared to a greying doxy guarding the roads from Limerick to Tralee. When I first saw her she was perfumed with booze and beefburger and bedecked with bunting as she played hostess to one of the many all-Ireland Fleadhanna held there.

As a refugee from the spiritual Chernobyl of Fermanagh, I found her warmhearted and gracious. She was welcoming and enticing. I vowed on our first meeting that I would eventually return.

Peter returned bearing Guinness.

"I was thinking about the man who wrote *The Boys of Wexford*" while I was waiting for the pints," he said. "It reminded me of the phase in Irish about Listowel. I can't remember the exact translation but it says something about Listowel being the grave of the native and the home of the stranger."

I was about to ask him to elaborate when the amplifiers burst into life.

"THIS IS WHERE THE COWBOY RIDES AWAY," the young man howled.

Peter glared balefully in his direction and moved his head closer to mine so that we could continue the conversation.

"It would break your heart that all the youngest, the brightest the best and are now waiting on tables in New York and San Francisco while at the same time young blackguards like that can manage to make a living here," he growled.

"Kerry can't even manage to scrape a half decent football team together. Once we could trounce the arse off every other county in the country, but look at the state of us now".

Coming from Fermanagh I felt it was wiser to say nothing.

"The whole fabric of Kerry is gone to Hell. You can walk down the street any morning and see well-to-do farmers walking into supermarkets to buy a four stone bag of spuds. They are too damn lazy and too gorged with Common Market grants to get up off their arses and plant a few ridges of spuds or a vegetable plot."

"The people of Tralee, Killarney, Dingle, Kenmare, Killorglin, and just about everywhere else would be starving if it wasn't for the tourists. The fishermen in Dingle have even forgotten how to fish since that bloody dolphin moved into the harbour. They spend their time taking tourists out to gawk and take photographs. By Christ, things have changed since I was a lad".

I ventured the opinion that anything was preferable to what was going on in my home county.

Peter was unrepentant. "We are so far removed from the seat of power down here that nobody cares about us. We are the forgotten county. The only people who really enjoy living here are outsiders like yourself who come in search of something that is impossible for the native to experience."

I had to admit that there was a lot of truth in that. It's one thing to have to live in a place and a totally different thing to have the ability to chose to live there.

For myself it was an easy choice. I was seduced not just by the endless grandeur of the place but also by its quirkiness and difference. The sea seems wilder here. The mountains more difficult to tame. The wide expanses of bog and moorland make a mockery of the gentle stretchmarks that mother Nature painted upon my own homeplace.

And that landscape has left its indelible thumbprint on the Kerry people. It has shaped and nurtured them in a way no other county has. They are truly a race apart; a people who treasure their diversity.

"DOWN BY THE BANKS OF THE OHIO," the young man howled in apparent desperation.

"I think," said Peter, "'Tis time to go."

I agreed.

The fresh air washed over us. As we walked up the street the sound of our bootheels bounced back from the ornate Pat McAuliffe shopfronts and faded in the strengthening wind.

"What other town in Ireland would have almost 60 public houses to cater for a population of just over 3,000 people," Peter challenged me.

"Cookstown," I replied, lying through my teeth.

"By Jaysus, they must be good drinkers up there as well," he chuckled in reply. "It's nice to know that we are not the only ones going to the bad."

We parted at the top of the town. I think that the last thing I said to him was that we would go off tomorrow and try to find the grave of the man who wrote *"The Boys of Wexford"*. He wound his way up the hill wafting clouds of Mick Mcquaid in his wake while I retraced my steps under solitary sodium shadow killers.

A wind that came all the way from the Gulf of Mexico hastened my steps. It carried fragments of music. While it might have been Daniel O'Donnell, somehow I feel that it just might have been *"The Boys of Wexford"*.

# By Dingle Bay and Blasket Sound

*Steve MacDonogh*

In Ballyferriter in Corca Dhuibhne
the Three Sisters rear their heads to look
out over the endless expanse of the sea.
In Ballyferriter in Corca Dhuibhne
cohorts of German boy scouts
shade their eyes towards Atlantic sunset;
beside them a gaggle of girls from Dublin
pile into the bus for the Dún an Óir.
No one grows up in Ballyferriter
without having one eye on the horizon
where sky meets sea and clouds roll in.
No one looks at the outline of the "Dead Man";
no one watches the light change in the west
of an evening that moves from blue to yellow,
from yellow to gold, to pink, red and purple;
no one watches or looks without knowing
that on the far distant shore of the ocean
lies a new destination, a life and a home
in a place that will never be home.
In Daniel Keane's a Corkman playes fiddle,
a Yank talks folklore and a Dub sings;
at the bar three local men in their sixties,
their eyes sinking misty into pints.
There are Spaniards in the Blasket Sound,
seized by the great mouth of the sea
from ships of the Armada;
Blasket and mainland fishermen too,
pulled to death before their time.
And now it is the air that plucks
the young of Ballyferriter
not to death but to exile
from the gateways of farewell

at Shannon, Cork and Dublin.
No one grows up in Ballyferriter
without having one eye on the horizon,
or an ear to the phone for news from beyond
from sisters, brothers, friends...
And in the lands of opportunity
young emigrants dream
of becoming anything they wish,
yet know the reality of the possible.
But "home," they say, "is the only place
you can just be yourself."
Home is the deep and healing well
to which they return; and here
they pay the round and dance
like pilgrims at an old pattern.
Few see the reasons for their exile,
few want to know, it being enough
to learn a new place in a new world.
At home it is only brochures
and bureaucrats that brag
about the wonders of deep ploughs;
the rest register vegetables
rotting on the dump or ploughed back,
register an industry of excuses
for management expenses.
The confident promontory forts
express a proud, developed past,
but their ruins watch over
seas whose produce is stolen
and fields where buachalláin buí
is the only crop.
The people of Duibhne are scattering
while wide-boys and apparatchiks
bray like satisfied donkeys,
reaping funds in the name
of heritage and co-operation.
Language is turned on its head:

money gives power to liars,
makes fools of true women and men.
No one grows up in Ballyferriter
without having one eye on the horizon
where sky meets sea and clouds roll in.

# Place and Displacement

*Clairr O' Connor*

My parents left home when I was fifteen. It wasn't unexpected
but it was still a shock. Home was Limerick. Limerick city. My
father said he was going home. Home to Listowel, Co. Kerry. Ever
since I could remember he'd been saying he would go home one
day. Perhaps I had heard it so often, I no longer listened. When
I was five he had said, "One of these days I'll go back. Limerick
is fine but it's not home. "Naturally I was confused. Limerick was
the only home I knew. Kerry was for the holidays. Ballybunion,
Stack's mountain, Listowel, daytrips to Tralee. My mother came
from Ballyalnan, a little village near Newcastle West, Co.
Limerick. Summer holidays were divided between Kerry and Co.
Limerick.

My parents boasted about the virtues of their respective
counties. Did this move to Kerry mean that my mother had lost?
An independent woman from a very early age, my mother left her
village after her Inter Cert. and went to England to train as a
nurse. A thrifty country woman she brought her rustic virtues to
a war-torn London making delicious meals out of meagre rations
to the delight of her city bred London nursing friends. On a visit
home to visit her widowed mother and her sister she met Ned
O' Connor on the train from Dublin to Limerick Junction. He
proposed to her some months later having first checked out her
Catholicity by writing to her parish priest in England. An almost
priest, my father has remained fervent to this day.

They married two years later. My mother returned to Ireland
to live. She got a nursing post in Limerick and my father worked
in Shannon Airport, the duty free section. Unlike most of the
women of my mother's generation, she continued to work outside
the home after she had children. Nursing was very important to
her. She was a meticulous homemaker as well. A splendid plain
cook, there was always a pot of home made soup available, brown

bread, scones, pies and special cakes for birthdays and Sunday teas. A woman of tremendous energy she applied her skills at home and at work. Her children's clothes were labelled and shelved. As a child, I both admired and felt intimidated by such order. As an adult I now realise that she probably insisted on such detailed order as a means of cutting off the criticism that was levelled at women who worked outside the home during the fifties and sixties.

I did not want to move to Listowel with my parents. I was in my Inter Cert year at school and pleaded impending exams as my excuse. But the truth was, I didn't want to leave the Shannon, my friends, the familiar geography of my existence; King John's Castle, Cannock's clock ringing the hours. I helped my parents pack and waved them Listowelwards with a smile. That night I howled my despair at their desertion into my pillow. I had got what I wanted but somehow I had lost. A hard one to figure. I had been left in the care of my aunt Mary until the end of the school year and my exams. Meanwhile my parents and my younger brother settled into the house in Convent Street in Listowel. I did not sleep that first night of their going. I hugged the night until dawn came. Then I got up and made a cup of tea. I trod warily, anxious not to wake my aunt.

I took down one of my grandmother's cups from the top shelf of the dresser. It was stark white with a decoration of a single bare branch of an oriental looking tree. This tea set was only used on Sundays. I felt a delicious sense of trespass as I drank thirstily from its restrained elegance. I thought if my grandmother (my mother's mother, Ita Nash) was here now I would be able to tell her of my confusion. She had lived with us until her death two years previously. She had been a playmate in spite of the generation gap. She allowed me to win at snakes and ladders and I enjoyed dressing up in her long dresses. A good musician, she played the fiddle, tin whistle and concertina. At family gatherings she played, my father and brothers sang and my sister and I danced reels and hornpipes.

As I sat there drinking out of the Sunday cup the morning after my parents' defection it suddenly came to me why my father had been harping on about going "home" to Listowel for years. When my grandmother had died two years previously I was so distressed that a few days after the funeral I decided to leave home. I was thirteen at the time. I talked to my best friend Breeda about it. She was Breeda with two ee's just as I was Clairr with two rr's. I wanted to go to Newcastle West and its environs, my grandmother's home territory. She had two sisters living within a six mile radius of each other outside the town. It was early January. I looked up the bus schedules and cashed in £5 of my post office savings and Breeda and myself headed for the country. I felt quite heroic. It was a stylish way to grieve, I thought — to go back to where my grandmother came from.

On arrival at our destination, I told the white lie that my parents knew where we were. There was still a week to go of the Christmas holidays from school. My relatives accepted my story. In that thoughtless way that children can, I did not think about the anguish my parents and Breeda's would go through when they discovered we were missing. I banished them from my mind and gave myself up to the moment. I rekindled my spirits at the open hearth, stamped my feet on the front door mat of the flagged floor kitchen as I came in and out like my cousins did. I watched my grand-aunt make bread and listened to her stories of when she and my grandmother were girls. There were tales of dances at the cross roads and house dances galore, matches made at harvest time and egg money put aside for material for dresses. I tried my best to be useful. I took my turn with the goose duster and polished the black range with zebrite. My grand-aunt liked to bake in a pot over the open fire but her daughter preferred the range. Three days into my runaway visit, my grand-aunt and her two daughters took the pony and trap into Newcastle West. They promised to bring me a bag of bull's eyes when they returned. They came back earlier than expected and in some agitation.

I learned that they had rung my mother at the nursing home where she worked. Sister had told them that Nurse O' Connor hadn't been at work for the past few days. Clairr and a friend had gone missing. My parents were in a terrible state. The gardai were doing their best but so far there was no sign of them. I was suitably mortified when my runaway status was exposed. Only then did the full seriousness of what I had done dawn on me. I wondered if we'd be sent back to Limerick in the pony and trap. But no. The Volkswagen was seen as a more speedy vehicle for our return. My grandmother's relatives did not scold us but it was clear that they thought we were "bold" for putting our parents through such needless worry. At home, I was greeted by a white-faced father and mother. According to my own logic, I explained I had to go away to be near my grandmother. My mother was furious. She said hadn't she enough trouble with her mother dying besides her daughter running off all in the same week.

My father said he could understand that I had wanted to be near my grandmother's relatives at a time like this. A daylong funeral wasn't enough at all to have a proper conversation with all of the people who had come for my grandmother's burial. If it had been in Kerry, the wake would have gone on for several days and I'd have been so exhausted at the end of it that I wouldn't have had either the energy or inclination to run off anywhere. I was grounded for months after that, only released from the supervision of the household for school and music lessons. I wrote letters to my dead grandmother in my journal (a hardbacked copy book) complaining about the unfairness of it all. I wrote her replies as well. She was on my side, of course. I wished that she could play me a tune to cheer me up.

As I drank from my grandmother's cup in my aunt's house the morning after my parents had left Limerick for Listowel, it occurred to me that my father was going home to Kerry to be with his own people just as I had followed my grandmother's people to Newcastle West after her funeral. Twenty years in Limerick had not made him a Limerickman. It had copperfastened his resolve to return to his home town. And so, he had taken early retirement from Aer Rianta and gone home to Listowel to open up a little bed and breakfast business. My father's mother, Katherine Kirby had died while still in her forties. Dead more than twenty years before I was born, obviously, I never met her. But from the earliest days she looked at me from photographs. Prim-featured, her hair always held under different hats, she looked at me and at the world as if she knew the measure of things. She played the piano well and married Bill O'Connor against her father's wishes. He charmed every woman he met. Or so the story goes. I have no recollection of meeting him.

After Katherine died, he married secondly and begat a large young family. My father and his sister Kathleen, lived with other relatives instead of in their father's house. Though my father has never said this to me, I think he must have had feelings of being dispossessed from that time. His need to go home to Kerry was a primitive one, to live again where his young romantic mother had played the piano for himself and his sister. Aunt Kathleen, my father's sister, died when she was twenty six. I never met her but I'm told I inherited her high instep but not her sweet disposition. In the mid sixties, when my father's stepmother emigrated to England, eight years after her husband's death, my father went home for good. He knocked the old house and built a modern one. The gate and yard face Convent Street and the garden overlooks the island where the Listowel races are held every September.

At various times in our early childhood, my brothers, sister and I had accompanied our father to the races in September. It was a wonderful feeling being released from the schoolroom when our Limerick friends where confined by school and its curriculum. The horses racing, the crowds, the town open for business were invigorating. We were treated to endless lemonade and chocolate. I brought home a leprechaun snowstorm and a cup and saucer embellished with shamrocks from one such outing. I bought them in one of those shops that sold everything from fertilizer to knitting needles. They cost six shillings and ninepence. And of course, there were my father's relatives pressing half crowns and even the odd ten shilling note into the hand.

We didn't visit his cousin Nora and her husband at Stack's mountain during race week. Stack's mountain was for the summer. Nora had no children but was amazingly tolerant of us and our soft city ways — like wearing shoes in the summer for instance. The children on Stack's mountain always went barefoot in the summer. I loved her griddle bread and potato cakes made over the open fire. Nora was unorthodox in her farming methods. The cows were often milked after darkness fell. Many a time she led me by the hand as her other hand held the storm lantern on our way to milk them. She never went to bed before midnight and often we were allowed to stay up to the witching hour with her. She read aloud Kitty the Hare stories from *Ireland's Own* to us, her face lit by the tilly lamp, her voice infusing the words with a terror and immediacy that I can still recall even today. We went to bed by candlelight. Those were the days before electricity had come to the mountain. Sometimes, as my candle flickered and my feet curled in anxiety under the eiderdown, I wondered if I'd survive until morning. I expected to be killed in my bed by one of the characters from Kitty the Hare.

Once, when I voiced this concern to Nora, she said, "Yerra girl, you could always bawl out loud, we'd surely hear you. Anyway, your guardian angel would see off any blackguard with a whip. They have special invisible whips made out of tough elastic. One belt of that and the blackguard would be sent screeching into the middle of next week." In the morning when the sun lit the high tongue and groove ceiling, I'd say a special prayer to my guardian angel for having seen off the night demons. Then, even before washing my face and hands with the pitcher of water on the bedside wash stand, I'd be off out to the fields. Sometimes, in the early mornings I would bring water from the well but I was always terrified of its dark depths. A neighbour's child had told me that a bad spirit lived in it and every few years the spirit grabbed a child and took it off to the black pit where it lived. I told myself I didn't believe the story but I never dawdled at the well, just in case. Running about the fields and hiding in the barn to read were my chief occupations. I collected the eggs and talked to Nora as she milked the cows. I was never bored and was always sad when leaving.

The first summer after my parents had gone to Kerry I felt peculiar going "home" to Listowel. It wasn't September, so there wouldn't be the races and I couldn't very well say I wanted to go to Stack's mountain since I hadn't seen my parents for some weeks. When I opened the yard gate and my brother Richard came to meet me yelling a greeting, I noticed immediately that his accent had changed. It already had touches of the Kerry lilt. My mother was cleaning the front windows. Indoors, in the dining room, my father was chatting to two American tourists. A middle aged couple. They were bronzed and outgoing. He was helping them pick out the next stage of their itinerary. I felt oddly piqued. Not only had my parents left home and come to Listowel, but they had settled in without any apparent transitional difficulties. My father was extolling the Bord Fáilte beauties of Kerry to this couple from Pennsylvania. I felt very left out of it all.

After a hasty greeting, my brother had headed off with some of his new friends to fish. My mother had made my favourite fruit cake for tea. She seemed happy and relaxed.

"Don't you miss nursing?" I asked her as I finished my second cup of tea.

"Of course I do, but they won't take me on in Tralee. Too old, they said. At forty eight! Over thirty years of experience doesn't seem to count for much. They don't approve of married women working, taking work away from young nurses. The same old chestnut! My thirty years experience doesn't seem to count for much."

"That's terrible," I encouraged her outrage.

"It is, " she agreed "but then life is often unfair. I'm angry but I'm not unhappy and that makes all the difference. We've settled in fine, as you can see and your dad's a new man. He plays the piano every day now. Still, if I get bored hanging about the house I'll find something else to do."

And she did. She got a job in the local cutlery factory. I thought she would find the work repetitive but she enjoyed the company of her workmates and made a new circle of friends.

She settled into her new life with vigour. The B & B side of my parents' life was busy during the summer months and the races during September. Later on, when Writers' Week became part of the yearly schedule, that was a busy week too. Writers and visitors came in and out of my parent's front door. Growing up in Limerick my father had bought Bryan Mac Mahon's books for us. They had been at school together, so he took a lively interest in his writing career. In our early teens he took us to see John B. Keane's *Sive* and *Many a Young Man of Twenty* when they came to Limerick. Now that my parents were living in Listowel, I met Bryan and John B. regularly. Bryan told me "There's at least one story inside everyone. If you can tell that story and get on to the next one, then you're a writer."

I thought of the journal I started to keep after my grandmother had died and wondered if that was a story but dismissed the idea. Real stories were published. I jotted things down in a journal, a hardbacked school copy. That wasn't the same thing at all. I was a reader, a voracious reader at that. I loved poetry. Palgrave's *Golden Treasury* was a favourite bag book. I had a system of reading which I adhere to even now. A bag book was the book I carried in my school bag. The book of the moment. The one I couldn't be parted from. A desk book was one that was meant to be elevating and improving. That summer and autumn of my parents' defection to Kerry, it was Simone De Beauvoir's, *Memoirs of a Dutiful Daughter*. I kept it in my desk in school covered in brown paper like the rest of my schoolbooks. Reading it made me feel I was in touch with European thought. A bed book was generally a biography. When I was fifteen it was a life of Shelley — "I fall upon the thorns of life, I bleed". A bathroom book — cartoons, comic novels. A travel book for trains and buses, usually plays. At that time it was Oscar Wilde's plays. I wished fervently I could live in one of his plays and be epigrammatically witty forever. "The General was essentially a man of peace, except in his domestic life." (Lady Bracknell).

Instead I was ill at ease and confused. Pressure was mounting or so I perceived it, for me to live in Listowel now that my Inter Certificate was over. I could go to the local convent and do my Leaving Certificate there. I resisted. Teenagers are always awkward at the best of times and I wasn't about to prove the exception. The bottom line was I felt my parents' defection to Kerry keenly but I refused point blank to join them. My parents were very patient and kind. They asked my aunt if she could put up with me for another two years of schooling and she agreed. I experienced simultaneously a deep sense of relief and also acute disappointment. I don't know quite what I had expected but as the summer progressed and I became familiar with the town, its square, its churches, the market I began to feel more at home there. I spent days in Ballybunion and got burned to a cinder. I walked the dog in Gurtinard and went on shopping sprees to Tralee with my mother.

My father had joined the church choir and sang lustily at as many masses as he could fit in. In Limerick he had sung plain chant, he now displayed tendencies towards ecumenism. He sang along at the new folk masses. He joined a prayer group and became a Padre Pio acolyte. The mixture of his old orthodoxy and his new evangelism confused me. I had grown up in a household in Limerick where to sing parts of the Latin mass was part of the normal recreation of the house. I could not remember a time before *Introibo ad altare Dei*, or *Domine non sum dignus*. Now he was singing along to "If you love Jesus, clap your hands." My mother was unperturbed. "He's loosening up, becoming less rigid. It's a good thing," she said. Just when I had become convinced that my parent's orthodoxy was a thing I was sure I could react against, it was being chipped away. In Limerick the rosary was said at a set time every evening. Now, my parents said it in bed, late at night. We could join them if we wished but it wasn't imposed. Initially I felt relief. After all, for years at the end of the rosary my sister Ita had prayed for the foreign missionaries, my brothers for new priests but my prayers were for virginity and the conversion of the Russians. As the summer wore on and I didn't join my parents for the rosary, when I heard their murmured voices in the distance I heard it as an exclusive mantra. A one which bound them together in their new life in Kerry. "Is praying in bed erotic?" I questioned my journal.

It wasn't until I had left school in Limerick and gone to college in Cork that I enjoyed in a natural way my holiday times in Listowel. By then, it was the norm for friends to go home at weekends to see their parents. It was the norm, not the exception. I began to see the warm side of my father's all embracing Catholicity. There was a festive air about the trips he organised to visit various religious shrines. My mother's home baking welcomed the prayer group which met at our house. My friends were always made welcome and my parents were never daunted no matter now many people I brought home. In time, my teenage resentment was healed.

After graduation and marriage, I moved to London for six years and I looked forward eagerly to coming home and spending part of my summer holidays with my parents in Listowel. Over the intervening years I had used Listowel as a base to explore other parts of the county. I particularly liked Dingle for its mix of cosmopolitan summer visitors while it retained the feeling that it's on the edge of the world. I wrote this poem there some years ago.


### *EDGE*

Richard says it's the most
westerly point in Europe
but today the mist is down.
Hard to believe they're mountains.
A cormorant whips the air.

No one on this beach but us.
One child ahead, marks
a trail the tide will take.

Another, determined, piles
stones. The last one
outraces waves on a borrowed
bike, a twilight bird.

Waves beat white light
to grey: clouds move
differently here, pushing
a way forward.
But rock pool crabs hide
when we pass.

I first came to Writers' Week in Listowel as a reader and a
buyer of books. Living in London, I felt it kept me in touch with
what was going on in Ireland and the *craic* was good. I usually
returned to London with a case of books. Fiction and poetry
mostly. My life in London was busy and full. I taught English in
a boys' grammar school in Harrow. Occasionally, in class, the
lesson taught and a few minutes to spare, I would read a poem
or story by a contemporary Irish writer, Eithne Strong, Eavan
Boland, Bryan Mac Mahon, Seamus Heaney. It made me feel a
part of the country I had left. I was proud of Ireland's writers,
glad to read them aloud to English schoolboys. I had no thoughts
of writing anything myself. I still kept the journal going, the one
I had started after my grandmother's death. By now it comprised
a rag-bag of numberless hardback notebooks filled intermittently
over the years with my thoughts on this and that.

My husband, Kevin and I returned to Ireland at the end of the
seventies. I got a teaching post in St Enda's Community School
in Limerick. Limerick, my first home. I was delighted. Kevin
wasn't as lucky. He couldn't get a teaching post to suit his subjects
in Limerick. He got a school in Dublin. We commuted for a year
but at the end of that year I realised it would be more likely that
I would get a school on the east coast than Kevin would get one
in Limerick. I resigned my teaching post in Limerick and signed
on to do an M.Ed course in Maynooth. I filled in several dozen

applications for teaching posts and eventually got one in Bally-mun Girls' Comprehensive School the following year.

It was in that summer of flux of 1979 that I signed on to do a poetry workshop at Listowel Writers' Week. The stipulation was that you had to submit five poems. There was nothing for it but to put pen to paper. At the time, I was angry at having to leave Limerick, having only so recently returned to it. My feelings about it triggered off the anger I had felt years ago when my parents left Limerick for Listowel. This is one of the poems I wrote.

### DREAM OF MY FATHER

It was his hand, a giant hand.
I was sitting in it, his thumb
my armrest. Market Day;
smell of fresh dung,
cows jostling with cars in the Square,
farmers in wellington boots and caps,
tomato complexions bruised from the wind.
The Protestant clock stuck at a quarter past ten.
He put me down among the stamping horses.
I did not cry.
Their hooves blocked out the sky.

I have lived in Maynooth Co. Kildare since autumn 1979. I had intended living here only for the duration of my M.Ed course, then we would move to Dublin. My son, Eamon was so happy in his pre-school in Maynooth that we didn't like to move and upset him as we were both working parents. By the time he had reached school age, he didn't want to live anywhere else. He's thirteen now, a Kildare man. And so, Kildare has become home.

In the summer of 1987 the B.B.C. recorded a ninety minute radio play of mine. It was called *Getting Ahead*. The play's main character was a principal of a school in Maggie Thatcher's England during the teachers' strike. I went to London for the recording. From there I travelled to America to an artist's colony to write. I had been given a scholarship by the Ragdale Foundation. My parents and my husband, Kevin were pleased for me.

In early December 1986, my mother had had a heart attack. She was critically ill. We thought she would die. My principal, Sean McCann (Coláiste Chiaráin, Leixlip) kindly arranged compassionate leave from school for me and I spent a week in the hospital with my mother. She was in the Bons Secours hospital in Tralee. I sat by her bedside in the intensive care unit by day and at night I slept in the children's ward. I did not want to leave her. I had to sleep in the foetal position to fit into the miniature bed. Occasionally, in the daytime, I would walk as far as the town centre just to get some air. The business and cheer of the Christmas shops upset me. Their jollity seemed tawdry. As she moved in and out of consciousness my mother was upset that she hadn't yet baked her Christmas cake. She tried to tell me the recipe but since she was a natural baker and never measured anything she couldn't tell me the proportions. Other times, she thought I was her mother and talked about her childhood in Ballyalnan, her home village. This is a poem I wrote about that time.

### LAST CHRISTMAS

For the first time, no arced fluid hands
throwing a pinch of this, a cup of that —
runic cooking for a family feast.

So changed from what I remembered.
Mother on her bicycle cycling towards
home, her nurse's veil winging the wind,
a lifetime of night duty behind her,
sending us to school with hot porridge
and brown scones inside us.

Her lips now whitened to a line,
unable even to hold water.

The nurses turn when she calls me
"mother". She promises to collect
the eggs, to clean the churns after school.

Her hands so still, so different
from the time I panicked at the crying
of my five day old son, not yet knowing
that children are survivors
handing him into her strong hands
glad she could be mother.

Amazingly, within six weeks she had recovered fully and was allowed home by the end of the following January. She continued to improve and sat out at home in the late spring sunshine. By early June when I left for England and America she was strong once more. My mother wrote me several letters while I was in America that summer. The last one she wrote did not contain the conventional address heading. It read simply "home". It was written a week before she died. It was early August, the turning of the year.

In the years since my mother's death, my father has been blessed by the company of his Listowel friends and relatives. Although living on his own, he is rarely alone. People pop in and out as they always did for a cup of tea or a chat. He tells my siblings and me not to worry about him. He's among his own people he says. You're supposed to be well-formed in character by the time you're fifteen, the age I was when my parents went to live in Listowel but I think that move had a profound effect on me. It deepened that inward questioning side of my nature which must contribute largely to the writer within. Place and displacement have shaped me. Even though I did not begin to write until my twenty-ninth year, I believe some of the significant experiences in my earlier life contributed to the writer I have become.

Growing up in Limerick, a city of walled fortifications, churches and a castle gave me a sense of the importance of history, a feeling that the city that had cradled me had played its part in resisting the colonists. I felt pride, a sense of belonging. Limerick is my first love. The name that springs to my lips when the question "Where are you from?" is asked. But since my late teens when I accepted Listowel as my second home, I have always added, "but my family moved to Listowel when I was fifteen." Now, after more than a quarter of a century travelling "home" to Kerry, I embrace its mountains and the sea around it and acknowledge its part in shaping me during those years.

In 1991, when my first novel, *BELONGING* (Attic Press) was published I was delighted when I was invited to launch it at Writer's Week in Listowel. Bryan Mac Mahon did the honours. In his speech, he talked about his long association with my family and praised the novel for its freshness and humour in handling such a serious topic as belonging, where a person felt they fitted in. Nora Relihan read several extracts from the book in that wonderful commanding voice of hers. When she finished, John B. Keane approached the microphone as he held my book aloft to the audience. He said, "You've heard Bryan Mac Mahon praise the book. You've heard Nora read from it. Now it's time to put your hands in your pockets and show your support for Ned O' Connor's daughter. I'm first in the queue to buy Clairr's book."

And he was. It reminded me of market day, where the seller hustles his customers into a bargain before they have time to change their minds. I was embarrassed but only momentarily. As I signed copies of my book, I was very glad of the warm reception.

# Kerry Talls and Tales.

*Lily van Oost*

"It is of no use to send your soul to search the vastness of the plains, the Tree of Truth does not wax there; nor will the wide winged progress of a bird reveal True Knowledge to you.

Do not, in your quest, strive at gauging the gyrations of our galaxy, because they are predestined by our Eternal Parent.

In one's quest for knowledge one shall not scrutinise the entrails of a sacrificial creature, nor attempt to read the sinkage of an exquisite cup of tea to seek the secrets of the future, not the crumbs of a savoury black-forest gateau. These ridiculous assertions are excerpts from the *Manuscript of Antimythology*.

How sad.

Isn't it pure magic to wallow through some sanguinolent intes tines with the aim of foreseeing the outcome of one's next orgical night out? If 't will be Mary instead of Molly, with Johnny instead of Paddy that we visit the licentious gooseberry bush.

An intimate moment of fervent introspection in a scatter of tea-leaves never harmed anyone, not even those more prone to reading Casey's *Forbidden Fruit, The Kerryman, Kerry's Eye* or *The kingdom*. Did I omit to mention the *Black Valley Gazette*? Well, it's because that one handles the news of the universe in a more oral than scriptural fashion.

How sad to see that some preachers, while gorging themselves with forbidden fruit, forbid them to us; oh, of all Kerry condoms! I am all for mythology, that is why I came to live here in the first place. The Kingdom of Kerry is full of fairies, myths ancient and myths new, spirits benevolent and spectres malevolent. Kerry is pregnant with *magie* and myths. Moths too if my neighbours let their fleeces tarry too long in the wool-shed!

Do you want a fair example; no, not of fairy moths, eejit, a mythologic example coming to us from the depth of time, when combs were still made of bone, not of gooey plastic as today.

At my arrival in Kerry, a couple of decades ago, I was warned never, *au grand jamais* never ever to pick-up a comb, out of sheer fear of the banshee, because these howling ladies of the night would haunt me for the rest of my dying days. And, thank you but no thanks, dear Banshees, my personal leprechaun stops by for tea and more, at the chimes of midnight. That's amply enough. To check the Banshee Myth I made a reserve experimentation by placing a comb in an obvious position, near my gate. A nice colourful, clean, vivid comb. Well that's years ago; the comb will soon take root as nobody touches it. It will still be there long after the ozone layer has disappeared, leaving us covered in oncologic melanomata. Brrrrr.

When I arrived in this Emerald Isle I was granted a good bit of information, on mighty myths. Here is a florilegium of tall Kerry Tales for your benefit:

1.—there are guaranteed no snakes in the place.

No wonder, says I, no wonder; how would a boa constrictor ever have a swum over from the tropics, or a viper from Westminster Parliament.

Another myth.

2.—there are a multitude of Irish saints.

What, says I, the Vatican recognises only one or two, and horror of all horrors, our national heroes Saints Bridget and Patrick are not even amongst them.

A third myth, a real tall one, this one:

3.—there is no sex in this country.

Remember, my friends, this assertion came to me twenty years ago, as I was settling down as a Kerryman - yes, correct, I said "Kerryman," nobody noticing was I a Kerry-man or a Kerry-woman.

This was alas in the bygone, saintly pre-bishopelian days. Ha ha. Mother Nature's cake got sliced a bit on the side, since. Even adultery is enjoyed nowadays, while in the good old times 'twas alright on condition that the perpetrators didn't enjoy "it".

Which was infinitely more decent, begorrah.

Every time I had a few jars at Bridie Courtney's pub — my local 50 miles up and down the Gap of Dunloe — I inquired about Irish pre-christian history. Patrons in distinct degrees of ascending inebriation assured me that before christianity hit the shores of yore there was no spirituality here, only Guinness and a drop of Paddy spirit. Horrible pagans infested the country. Paganism was a highly reprehensible sun- and moon-worshipping, a figmentative monkey-chacha practised by our fore-mothers and monkey-daddies in the tree of life.

Yggdrasil.

Figmentation.

Fig leaves...

I soon knew that Irish catholicism differs from the Roman Catholic and Apostolic religion. What was the root of this anomaly?

Maybe because it fed from pagan rooting-compost, differing from euro-compost because of the characterised insular geography of this blessed emerald isle.

Trying to know more about Irish paganism proved impossible. An unscrutinisable shroud of silence blanketed the millenniae. I suppose the subject was anxiously kept off the school rostrum as inspired non-bearded bards might otherwise emerge from the ranks of our prepubescent innocenti.

Brrrr....

Or druids come forth, from between the school-benches.

Or worser than worse: that sculptors and painters would be ignited by those horribly obscene fertility-goddesses, the Sheilas... or Sheel-na-Gigs'n'Reels. These carnal monstrosities are luckily safely kept in solitary confinement in the vaults of the

National Museum, in the deepest caves Dublin Corporation ever dug. One needs a vaticanese dispensation or at least be a bishop to gain access to the erotic carvings.

Potential spectators are strongly encouraged instead to diddle on the ground floor, amidst Cuchulain's fancy golden Channel-cufflinks, his elegant golden Costelloe-lunulae, preciously designed Armani-torques; or to admire the gorgeous Ardagh chalice; or consult a page of the one third of the Book of Kells — the other turds, pardon my French, the other thirds being in TCD and in the Chester Beatty Library (if not "cleansed" by our manuscript-kidnapper extraordinaire).

Meanwhile...restless, deep down are the fertility-goddesses, far below the warriors' weaponry, cloaks and daggers, the lacy frills, the parchemin calligraphy.

Deep.

Deep down, indeed.

Deep in us, and very much alive alive-ho, is the rich ancient tradition, the lively layer of Irish mythology.

It was impossible for me to settle down properly without knowing more about the sources that make Ireland so Irish. So, I started digging and soon had a panoramic history-oversight:

— In 6,000 B.T.T., BEFORE OUR TIME-TELLING, thus 8,000 years ago, after the last ice-age — I hope — the sea rose high enough to separate us physically from Britain. Then Britain was cut-off from Europe — and, as today's Thatcherites go, they have no intention of closing the gap; the Channel tunnel is sabotaged in every way possible. The French are having great fun; while they are ready with their T.G.V. or *Train á Grande Vitesse*, to link Paris to London in no time, the English aren't. But in true British strait-face tradition they'll have in Dover, at the disposal of the Continental pressé-passengers, modern mauve four-geared bicycles to help the traffic to London and further on to Kerry. This tunnel-tale has nothing to do with mythology, but I couldn't resist volunteering this information.

— So now, let's get on our bike and return a couple of millenniae *en arriére.*

Just as we (let me say "we" because I got full Irish citizenship) were becoming an island, the first aborigines arrived, originating from Scandinavia. When these gatherer-hunters had degustated every elephant and elk around they got a problem: they were stuck for food, mammoths don't regenerate spontaneously.

During the epoch that elephant-and-elk steaks had been dished up in the Irish Elm and Mistletoe Café, the first farm-estates were being instituted in faraway Mesopotamia — the cradle of our civilisation. Soon this trendy way of life spread towards Europe and beyond.

Our forebears hadn't sat still during their hard times, they built gigantic ceremonial and burial monuments in Kerry and else- where, many of which, still unexplored, keep their secrets within their entrails, behind virginal vulval entrances made of huge blocks erected under the abracadabra direction of the druidic architect *en vogue* in those days.

—In 3,000 B.T.T., the neolitho-colonialist Euro-Farmers, des-perately in search for more arable turf, landed here. They meta-morphosed Ireland into an agro-business-minded country. While we know little of their culture and less of their pre- decessors', we know of a thriving export of axes made of polished stone fixed on a wooden handle. May this be an inspiration for us, to solve the current recession.

— In 2,000 landed on our shores metalworkers and prospectors probing for ore, copper and gold, of which there was plenty in the early-bronze-age. The axe-trade was overtaken by export of mun-ificent golden and copper artifacts, weapons, ornaments and vessels. They leave a glorious taste of Ireland all over Europe.

—2,500 years ago, iron-workers established themselves in Europe, who all too soon manufactured the Rolls-Royce of all Chariots of Fire. The axe was replaced by more lethal military weapons. Consequently, decimating wars spread like brushfire.

— 2,000 years ago arrived the Celts, our most glorious ancestors, who played a key-role here, lasting a millennium and whose inheritance still produces its fruits.

Their tribal name is primarily a linguistic term dictated by their common language. As Greek and Sanskrit, Celtic or Keltic is of Indo-Euro origin. The Irish language derives from a "dialect" called Q-Celtic...and is thus much older than our vile and common modern English. Tá sé go dona — pardon my Irish.

The Kelts had spread from the Orient into the Near-East and the Continent. In their progression they permeated their culture with local elements which we inherited: a goldmine of myths, creeds, traditions, in which we only had to dig our metaphysic denture.

—From Mesopotamia in Iraq originate the Gilgamesh Myths: written 6 or 7,000-years ago in the first human script, Sumerian, engraved in clay tablets. Yes, the very same we helped bombard with Allied precision-bombs during the Gulf-War — our contribution to civilisation.

Simply implanted onto the original myths by Palestinian roadside-rabbis, the Gilgamesh Myths were metamorphosed into the biblic old testament, yes, your very bible.

—The itinerant Kelts brought us another snake-cult than Adam's, namely that of Pythia, the Delphi snake-goddess. The snake, later so abhorred and repressed by the Vatican, is the intemporal symbol of Wisdom and Knowledge.

Goddess Pythia has power over life and death; see, yearly she sheds her skin — some will say "geansai" — only to start anew without further ado and meanders sinuously along the philosophical labyrinth of conscience and inconscience.

The Celts replaced the stripper-snake by a beast nearly as interesting, namely the beloved winged dragon so well illustrated in the cartoons of the Book of Kells. Catholicism soon saw the utility of this Celtic creature, *sito presto* incorporating it in its rites. A companion, Saint George, now keeps Python under constant surveillance, but the lad is in big trouble with Green

-peace, accused of dragon-slaying. Apropos, I don't know if St. George got a union-card as an homologised saint.

Ah, well...

My curiosity in matters past increased forcefully when I saw "my" first ogham stone, in solitary erection on a Black Valley hill. Now my thirst for knowledge became unquenchable and while bookinising voraciously I found a photograph of the famous stone of TUROE, Turoe being a town in a county very much in the news nowadays because it lost a bishop to sexual rites. The Iron Age stone offers striking similitude to the Delphi stone called the NAVEL OF THE WORLD.

Both are ogham stones by nature: their primeval energy strongly sourced in the sexual symbolism of the lingam, that macho appendix being mandatory to all patriarchal persuasions, from Asian-Indian to Christian creeds.

Pythia surely inspired the carvings decorating the phallocratic shape, as if the sculptor had retraced in stone the movements left in the sand by Monty Python's travails.

Our ancestors erected hundreds of boisterous phallic ogham stones in Ireland. While the Sheela-na-gigs were considered offensive to the vociferous prude, the giant condomised inflatables aren't!

Oh, mythic male fallacy.

Oh, obstreperous misogyny!

(Let me use this expression, I love it.)

Some ogham stones were edged with Runen-signs, which must be read from bottom to top... A *magnifique* example is the neat row in my parish, Lios na Phúca, in a site barely half a mile beyond our three Beaufort pubs.

Now listen; if, after hours, you see someone laying flat out by said stones, believe me, it's out of undiluted literary motivation; an intellectual spread of the purest water, in our own mini-Stonehenge.

The mysterious mystic spirals, lozenges, circles, intricate geometric patterns, certainly obeying strict rules of the period, are repeated in may neolithic constructions. Instigated by snake and sun movements, they inspired and continue to inspire artists of all disciplines.

—Returning to my panoramic view of Irish history I can't resist reminding you that Belgium had something to do with it. On a sunny day, long before I invaded the Black Valley, a Belgian tribe, the Menapiërs, sailed from Bruges into Wexford Harbour. They were later seen in Ulster, flagging the alias Fir Manach. One or other of the dreaded Fir Bolg, or rather Fir Flemings, must be my ancestor.

—From the years 700 to 800 on, due to increasing language maniability, Irish history became more readily recordable — Celtic being the vernacular lingo, Latin reserved for scripture.

Irish Christianity, that landed here just before the VI century, was rapidly the most worthy export to the Continent, greatly enriching mediaeval intellectual values. A string of Irish Euro-universities was established, many still prospering today; the facts were accurately recorded for prosperity.

—I'll get off my bike, leaving the past by only briefly mentioning a few painful events : Viking Imperialism that gave Brian Boru so much trouble in the X century; the Anglo-Norman terror occurring in the XI and XII centuries; English Imperialism that annexed Ireland as a colony in 1300; the Black Death cruelly striking the island in 1348.

I bear in mind all the horror and terror before and after the Great Famine of 1845, you, the Irish-born, know those facts so much better than me. But I personally witness the present day obscenity of the island's division, a colonialo-christiano-financial drama causing so much misery and death on both sides. Happily a glimmer of hope has risen since our President, Mary Robinson, had tea in Buckingham Palace with the British Queen, Elizabeth II, just a while ago.

Irishness means resilience and, however hard the times were, people never lost their sense of wit, mirth and myths. Many ancient beliefs and practices are kept very much alive, besides the Banshee comb's one. The druidic association with holy oak and parasiting mistletoe permits us to kiss anyone we fancy, that's if we have our timing and mistletoe-location right.

Right?

Three thousand sacred Irish wells, one of them two-millenniae-old, are still arduously visited by disciples of the Water Goddess, sometimes called Coventina. The custom of hanging strips of clothing by a holy well is still practised, although the church has tried to erase from christian memory the connection with the Mother-Goddess whom it is actually we adulate. There is nothing wrong with venerating mother earth and holy water. We should keep alive the beneficial, generative forces of Nature - with a majuscule N to her Name.

The pre-Celtic, the Celtic shaman, was the embodiment of our psyche, and will linger on with us, that's if we don't ingest too many soap-operas. The quest for the spiritual, the inner search, is aborted by the venomousness we presently vegetate in: artificiality, noise — food — toxicity — substances...preponderance of constant lazy choices of the lowest common denominator. This lifestyle is pure murder of the mind — our mind, our most precious treasure.

The readily and slavish acceptance of telegenic aggressivity is a major contributor to the degenerative process we have engaged in. Let's in heaven's sake waive away our phallocratic millions-and milliards-worth of missiles.

If we feel the compulsion to go to war, then by all means, let's do it in artistic fashion, by shedding our clothes and in the ancestral Picts and Celts tradition, storm the battlefield, our body painted all over with awe-inspiring dragons, multicoloured spirals, what have you. Let's scream like mad, run about turbulently, agitatedly whisk our axe at arm's length, to frighten the living daylight out of our *enemy-du-jour* (our yesterday's friend and tomorrow's ally).

In doing so we will consume so much energy by the time our *myopic* eyes cross those of our potential enemy we are no longer able to lift a finger, certainly not to slash him. We might even die in an irrepressible fit of ribald laughter.

So much for suicide.

If, miraculously, we survived the high-spirited battleaxe games, and as the vapours of peace descend upon the thatched cottages, we'll carnally sink — still covered in body-paint — by the fire, and sweat it out in a...shall we say...more sensuous way, for the furthering of future generations.

After that we'll fall in a reparatory sleep and dream of more magic practices drawn from the collective subconscience.

Why not have a reverie about the quadrature of holy trees: rowan, holly, elder and whitethorn; discover Amerikay in a second Navigatio Brendani; heave the Puck-Goat on his Killorglin pedestal. Having oniric difficulties with milk-churning, why not thrust into our recalcitrant milk — surely as a last resort — a dead man's hand, and see: in a sure state of shock the cream will quickly rise her peaks to the beam by the spidery loft.

Another suggestion, unconnected with aforementioned churning business except for the rising agent: why not join a funeral party. Remember the positive aspect: there will be one less drunk there than at a wedding party, with him laying in the coffin and all. Bear in mind that, due to certain sexuo-funereal practices, some rightout obscene, more matches are made at wakes than at weddings.

For the funeral proper we shall not forget to position on the corpse, already dressed in his last wooden suit, a plateful of tobacco or salt and even a brick of turf, to prevent early putre faction, or if this word makes you feel squeamish shall I put it as "*disintegratio praecox*"? *En passant* we must not forget to shake the chairs on which the coffin had rested, to expel the devil and his scythe from the room.

We may now let the dead rest in peace, the poor fellah having enough trouble as it is, facing the daisies and the worms the wrong way up.

Why not join another of those glorious occasions which provide excellent excuses to legitimise workplace absenteeism. And what is more appropriate after a wake than to dream of a wedding where we'll dance till morn. Why not invite the maiden of the mountain to perform the suggestive broom-dance which reads more clearly than the best sex-manual in the west.

If we are unlucky in matters of the heart we consult the book of Kerry Charms. And here is the cure: a strip of skin removed from a corpse and wrapped around our beloved's wrist is a potent love-charm. You see now that we had to go to a funeral first, in order to make matters of the heart work out. A piece of advice: wait till the object of your desire is sound asleep before you perform the skin-graft lest you lose your last chance. Then, when the beloved is under the grafted spell, walk her to a holed stone and, to seal the bond forever and thereafter, clasp your hands through the hole — only the hands, mind you, lest you alienate the gods of fertility.

But, if infertility is in the air, do visit "Granna's bed", the old stone whereupon it is advised to make love. Sometimes couples prefer to fornicate on the backseat of a car, which is also known to be pregnancy-conducive.

Once we have regulated the Miscellany of Kerry Magic to the shelf of our subconscience we slowly return to the real world. Leaving our crowded dreams for the next booze'n'snooze, we jump out of our bed, careful not to get caught in our oniric Keltic tomahawk and pots of Pict paint. After mentally washing the bodypaint away we are now fully awake and energised, all set to perform our daily task. The artists amongst us will paint, write, compose, magnetised by a breath of fresh air and by our crowded valise.

We are not alone.

The past, present and future are with us. We have our claws and roots firmly dug in our rich, imaginatory and real, systolic and symbolic world.

Many people still ask me why I settled down here for good. But is it a wonder that somebody like me instantly fell in love with Kerry, and why I immediately grabbed the chance when it miraculously presented itself: to get a cottage in the remotest part of the Kingdom. After becoming irredeemably sick of overcivilisation in my beautiful but oh so stressed and pragmatic flat Flanders I wanted to kiss every Blarney and ogham stone, to climb each range, to laugh at every salmon showing off her teeth on her way to her breeding-grounds up the battered Kerry cascades.

Is it a wonder that I immediately transferred my tools to my humble cottage, now furnished with drawing tables and painters' easels and typewriters and with all the silence of the world, so conducive to creativity.

Is it not normal that I surrounded my Kerry atelier with glorious semi-tropical vegetation which shows her enthusiasm by prodigally projecting her emerald luxuriance towards me and towards all creatures choosing to clock their heart in unison with mine. From my Kerry-jungle full of animals and flowers I direct my unpolluted artist's antenna at the universe.

*En passant*, my neighbours give me a golden smile; a dog barks, a sheep chews a daisy, the house is warm, the rain soft, streamlets and rivulets draw silver lines on the mountain-face with their peaks clad in mushrooming mystic clouds.

A chasing cormorant breaks the mirror of a lake, hardly disturbing a couple of majestic swans, overlooked from afar by a rare planing eagle...all is harmony.

Not so far away, though, reigns manmade horror.

Wars, Belfast, Bosnia, Somalia, Oil-land, the destruction of our globe, our one and only mother earth...wicked actuality is not whisked away from my beloved Black Valley.

From my atelier, afflicted by the barbarism of our civilisation, but also out of gratitude for the things of beauty that still remain, now armed with some understanding of the Irish pagan past, with all I learned on the Continent, constantly updated with the depravity of some of our globo-leaders, I work like mad, bearing witness to bad and good, screaming...on my paper.

spit of anger
fire of speech
breath of knowledge
line at the bitter edge
of the sword of wisdom
colour of a swansong
the flight of a bird
thunder and passion
a storm in a teacup
banshees buzzards
mountains and vales
the world is ours
to destroy or to love.

# Faoi Dhraíocht

*Nuala Ní Dhomhnaill*

Is le madra mallaithe a bhí againn thall i Sasana a chuala an ainm á lua ar dtúis; brocaire gorm darb ainm "Kerry". Ní raibh de chlaisceadal á chlos agam gach lá ach "Come here, Kerry!" "Go home, Kerry," "Go on awy out ou're that, Kerry". Bhí an "Kerry" céanna asa mheabhair glan. Do réab sé a raibh roimhe. Do chreim sé a chró féin is gach doras is geata a bhi san áit. Do dhein sé ciota fogha den ngairdín. Bhíos sceimhlithe im' bheathaidh roimhe. Ar a shon san is eile níl mar a déarfá aon chuimhne cheart agam air. Ní cuimhin liom an raibh sé mór no beag, reamhar nó tanaí, cé go gcloisim fós gach ní,—fuaim a chuid creimnithe mar fhrancach san oíche, gíoscan an tslabhra lena mbíodh sé ceangailte is an tafann, an síor thafann riamh is choíche. Ní lú ná mar is cuimhin liom cad a tharla dó sa deireadh. Lámhachadh é, ní foláir. Níorbh aon díobháil. Go binn a bhí sé tuillte aige. Bhí an chroch rómhaith dhó.

Bhínn ag cur na ceiste i gcónaí cad ba chiall dá ainm "Kerry". Dúradh liom toisc gur "Kerry Blue" ab ea é. Gur ó Chiarraí a tháinig sé. An áit úd in Éirinn gurb as mo mhuintir. Gur tháinig m'athair is mo mháthair is Nóirín a bhí ag tabhairt aire dhom ó Chíarraí. Go mbeimíst ag imeacht ann seara fada; —"going to Kerry". Cheapas-sa gur ag dul go dtí an gadhar ab ea é; - "I don't want to go to Kerry". Thitidist timpeall an urláir ag gáirí fúm. Áit ab ea an Ciarraí seo go rabhamair ag dul chuige, ní gadhar. Níor thuigeas-sa cén sórt ainmhí é áit. Nó b'fhéidir gur thuigeas ach nach cuimhin liom anois gur thuigeas. Tá na rudaí seo go léir meascaithe suas fós im' cheann agam.

Ní hea nach rabhas tar éis bheith ann cheana, is faoi dhó leis. Tráchtann m'aintin May fós ar an lá a chonaic sí m'athair is mo mháthair ag teacht aníos an pábhaille ón nGeata Beag is an t-amhas seo de ruidín beag rua ag siúl eatarthu istigh. Mise a bhíonn i gceist aici. Bhíos fiche éigin mí d'aois. Níor thuig sí gurb

78

ann dom go dtí an nóiméad sin. Más fíor. Nó conas gur féidir leis a bheith amhlaidh? An ea nár scrígh an bheirt deirféar chun a chéile i rith an ama? An é sin a chiallaigh bheith ar deoraíocht thiar ins na caogadaí, ná cuirfeá in úil do do mhuintir age baile an raibh leanbh agat nó an rabhais beo no marbh? Tá's agam nách raibh mo mháthair ach díreach tagaithe amach as an ospidéal tar éis luíochán bliana de bharr drochthaom eitinne, ach ba dhóigh leat go mbeadh scéala éigin curtha abhaile aici. Bhí, is dócha, ach ní cuimhin liomsa é. Tá na rudaí seo go léir meascaithe suas fós im' cheann.

Pé ar bith scéal é is cumhin liom go dianmhaith an samhradh go rabhas a trí is go rabhas sceimhlithe roimh an madra agus go rabhamair ag dul go Ciarraí seara fada. Is cuimhin liom gach nóiméad dó. Ar dtúis chaitheamair dul go cathair mhór Learphoill. Bhí greim docht ar láimh m'athar agam. Bhí sé ag siúl síos is suas, síos is suas an ché, dhá thruslóig á thógaint agamsa in aghaidh coiscéime amháin leis siúd. Theaspáin sé dom dealbh an éin mhóir a bhí thuas ar barr an fhoirgnimh ab airde san áit. B'sin é an "Liver Bird" as ar hainmníodh "Liverpool". Mar ar ainmníodh an gadhar "Kerry" as an áit go rabhamair ag dul ann. Nó an slí eile thart. Nó an slí eile thart arís. Ó ba chuma. Is cuma. Pé scéal é tá na rudaí seo go léir meascaithe suas im' cheann agam. Bhí droichidín caol adhmaid nó stangairt le dreapadh suas air chun dul ar an mbád. Ní raibh an ceann ag dul air ró-olc mar bhí sé déanta de phlancanna adhmaid is ní raibh aon radharc agat ar an bhfarraige ag drannadh thíos fút. Ach an ceann ag teacht anuas den mbád ar an dtaobh eile, bhí sé déanta d'iarainn agus bhí poill mhóra ann agus bhí radharc tríothu i bhfad thíos fút ar an bhfarraige cháite ag géimneach is ag coipeadh is ag féachaint le leanaí beaga a shlogadh. Ansan bhí moill fhada éigin i dteach na gcustam. Málaí agus cásanna á n-oscailt is á ndúnadh. M'athair ag siúl síos is suas, síos is suas ina bhróga móra buí go raibh poill bheaga ionntu. Mise ag sodar taobh leis, mo láimh fós ina láimh siúd. Dhá thruslóig seo'gamsa in aghaidh na haon coiscéime aige siúd. Cad a bhí á smugláil againn ins na cásanna? Stocaí níolóin agus gléasanna freacnarcacha anall ó

Shasana? Nó arbh é an slí eile thart é, agus gur ag tabhairt
bágúin is im is bia maith na hÉireann linn a bhíomair, ar an slí
thar n-ais go Sasana, áit a raibh cúpóin chiondála fós i réim? Ní
cuimhin liom. Bhíos ró-óg. Tá na rudaí seo go léir fós meascaithe
suas im' cheannn.

Sa deireadh do scaoileadh linn agus b'eo chun siúl sinn. Bhí
aistear fada ar thraen romhainn agus ag deireadh an aistir bhí
tollán mór dorcha a chiallaigh Corcaigh. Cúpla lá ansan agus
aistear ghluaisteáin ansan a thóg tráthnóna iomlán chun gur
shroiseamar an tigh ar an bPaddock, i mBaile Móir, laistair de
Dhaingean, agus crónú na hoíche ann agus an líon tí go léir
bailithe isteach sa chistin ag rá na Corónach. Mo Neain in éadaí
dubha na baintrí agus í ar a glúine thuas ar chathaoir shúgáin,
an chuid eile acu bailithe timpeall uirthi, m'úncailí agus Sean-
Mhaurus, mo shean-úncail, a chaipín píceach casta droim thar
n-ais ar a cheann. Bhí adhmad uile an tí ag glioscarnach faoi
bhrat nua péinte mar bhí na Stáisiúin chughainn aon lá anois.
Dathanna páipéar milseán a bhí ar an bpéint, buí is gorm is
bándearg is glas éatrom na n-úll. Smuirt láidir de a chaitheamh
anuas ar pé dath a bhí ann ón mbliain roimhe. Obair a deineadh
mar a deintí gach aon rud eile sa tigh sin d'aon turrag buille
amháin agus faoi dheabhadh. Bhí an péint fós gan triomú i
gceart. Bhí naithreacha beaga ag sníomh tríd, go háirithe ar an
mbalastráid. Bhí na naithreacha fós bog. Ba é an mian ba mhó
im' chroí ná mo mhéireanta a shá síos iontu go dtí an péint a bhí
mós beag fliuch. Ba é an crá is mó ar mo chroí ná lobháltaí dom
é is go mbítí ág tabhairt amach dom as bheith ag priocadh anseo
is ansiúd air i ngan fhios d'éinne, mar a cheapas.

Nuair a thagamais anuas an staighre ar maidin bhíodh
créatúirí de shórt eile ag dó na geirbe ionainn. Bord mór na
cistineach agus é ina bheatha glan le portáin is le gliomaigh is
piardóga mór cráifise. Mo bheirt uncail, Seán agus Eoghan — nó
Na Lads mar a thugadh gach éinne orthu-, a bhí tagaithe isteach
ó bhiaiste na maidne ag tarrach photaí. Bhí a raibh fachta acu
fós ina mbeathaidh agus iad ag lamhancán ar fuaid an bhaill.
Chonac na créatúirí ciotarúnta amscaí ina steille-mbeathaidh ó

bharr an staighre ach thíos ar an dtalamh bhí an bord ró-ard dom agus ní raibh aon radharc cóir agam orthu. Daoine am ardú suas ansan, ag breith ar ghliomach dom, á chraitheadh suas lem phus, á dteaspaint dom, á gcomhaireamh dom;—"triopal treapal, carraig a' rascail, cé méid gliomach atá ag an rí? Ceann inniu is ceann inné is dhá cheann déag ag siúl an tí." Ní cuimhin liom níos mó cad a tharla dóibh. Tugadh 'on Daingean iad chun iad a dhíol, is dócha. Ní dóigh liom gur i itheamair aon cheann riamh díobh. B'fhéidir gur dhein. Ní cuimhin liom. Tá na rudaí seo go léir fós meascaithe suas im' cheann.

Ach tá cuimhne ghléineach agam ar Na Lads iad féin. Seán, a bhí ina Chaptaen san Airm, agus ar an bhfoireann mharcaíochta sa Churrach, bhí ceann ciardhubh air, gruanna dearga agus fiacla gléineacha. Déarfá Naoise leis nó duine éigin do laochra óga na Féinne. Agus bhí sé muinteartha, leis, agus an-mhaith le leanaí. Ar a lá breithe féin, Lá Sin Seáin, do chuaigh sé amach sa ghairdín ar thaobh an tí liom is do rug sĭsiúirín leis is do ghearr sé na deilgeanna anuas des na róiseanna dom chun go bhféadfainn pósae dóibh a bhaint agus a thabhairt dó dá lá breithe. Ghlac sé an bronntanas uaim go mómharach is ansan bhronn thar n-ais arís orm é le gach onóir. Bhíos-sa ins na flaithis, im' choda beaga timpeall air leis an nóitis ar fad a bhíos ag fáil uaidh, agus é chomh breá san. Eoghan ansan, an mac ba shine, é siúd a bhí ag fanacht age baile is ag fáil na talún, gruaig chasta rua a bhí air siúd. D'iarr sé orm lá an dtiocfainn suas an cnoc leis i ndiaidh caorach. D'fhág sé i lár bearnan mé is dúirt liom aire na fola a thabhairt dó is gan ligint d'aon chaora dul isteach sa ghort, ach mo léir, nuair a chonac na caoirigh chugham ina dtréad ag méileach, agus gach ceann acu nach mór chomh mór liom féin agus níos mó b' fhéidir, sea, d'fhágas an bearna baoil agus do theicheas. Bhí Eogan an-chneasta liom nuair a thuig sé nách raibh ionam ach gearrachaille beag cathrach, a rá is go mbéadh eagla orm roimh scata caorach. Thóg sé suas ar a ghualainn mé is thug marcaíocht síos an cnoc dom agus isteach abhaile. Sea is cuimhin liom go maith Na Lads, a gheallgháirí is a bhíodar is conas ná fanaidís riamh socair, bhí útamáil éigin is tarractríd is

81

pléaráca éigin ar siúl timpeall orthu i gcónaí. Is cuimhin liom lá an mheithil, bheith ag féachaint anuas orthu ó fhuinneog na binne sa seomra codlata mar ar cuireadh mé as an slí ins an tranglam. Bhíodar beirt seasta in airde i lár stácaí leathnna coirce, agus na punainneacha á gcaitheamh suas ag daoine eile chuthu. Ansan dheinidís mar a bhéadh stúca istigh ina lár mar dhíon ar an rud ar fad. Stácaí sceimheal a chuala á thabhairt ar a leithéidí i bhfad i bhfad ina dhiaidh sin agus n'fheaca in aon áit eile á ndéanamh iad ach thoir sa Phaddock. Na Lads seasta istigh i lár an stáca choirce tráthnóna samhraidh is an ghrian ag buíú is ag dul i bhfarraige as an spéir siar ó dheas uathu. Tranglam agus béiceanna agus liúnna gáirí san aer. An obair ag dul ar aghaidh ar dalladh faid is a mhairfeadh an aimsir bhreá.

Is do bhíodh an aimsir breá, ní speabhraoidí ná díchuimhne faoi ndeara mé a cheapadh. Bhíodh leoithne bheag ghaoithe ann i gcónaí, toisc go raibh an tigh ar an ard os cionn na farraige ag béal an chuain, a aghaidh siar aduaidh treasna an pharóiste. Bhíodh an leoithne ghaoithe seo ag séideadh agus sinn ag siúl Faill na gCaorach siar tráthnóna, mise agus mo mháthair is na seanchairde scoile a tagadh á féachaint anois nó bhí sí tagtha thar n-ais ó Shasana. Bhíodh paróiste uile Fionntrá ag leathadh amach ó siar ó thuaidh uainn treasna an Chuaisín, is thall ar an dtaobh eile den gcuan bhí Cathair a' Treanntaigh mar a raibh m'aintín Máire pósta agus an Ché go mbíodh na Lads ag iascach as. Ach anois ba leor dúinne a raibh timpeall orainn; - bláthanna bána agus bándearga an rabháin a dtriomú sa bhríos briosc; mise á mbailíu i dteannta na nóinín mór is na nduán caorach; mo Mhaim go gealgháireach ag caint lena cairde, nó iad ag scigmhagadh is ag déanamh leibhéil ar an radharc faoina mbun thíos, áit nach dóchúla ná riamh go raibh mo Dhaid ag snámh roimis, an stróc brollaigh á dhéanamh aige go breá fada mall binn réidh, é os cionn a bhéime in uiscí ciúine an chuaisín ghlais. Ba dhíol iontais a leithéid i mbaile iascaireachta, áit nach raibh buile snámha ag éinne. "Féach thíos fúinn é" a chloisim ma mná ag seitreach, "níl aon oidhre eile sa domhan mhór air ach frog." Agus bhí an ceart acu. Mar sin go díreach a bhíodh an snámh ag na froig go mbeireadh sé orthu ina lámha agus é ag réabadh an ghairdín thall i Sasana. Thugadh sé isteach sa seomra níocháin mé is chuireadh sé isteach i ndamhach uisce dom iad chun go bhféadfaimist beirt an cumas snáma acu a iniúchadh go cruinn. Is cuimhin liom lá ar bharr na haille go rabhamair ag féachant romhainn amach mar sin. Do tháinig bean amach as tigh beag treasna an Chuaisín, áit a mbódh daoine muinteartha linn, na "Cúisins" ina gconai tráth go dtí gur ardaíodar a seolta leo go Denver, Colorado is gur dhíoladar an talamh. Do shíuil an bhean seo amach as tigh agus fan barr na haille siar agus gúna samhraidh cadáis uirthi is an sciorta leathan air á shéideadh in airde sa ghaoth. Níorbh aon ní é sin, mar ba é seo tréimhse na gcaogadaí luatha, nuair a bhíodh burla maith éadaigh le caitheamh le gach sciorta mar fhreagra ar an ngorta éadaigh aimsir an chogaidh. Ach sé a dhing an radharc seo im' chroí i slí nach ndearmhadfaidh mé riamh é ná go raibh gearrachaille beag ag sodar ina diaidh aniar, cailín comhaos liom fhéin b' fhéi dir, agus an gúna ceanainn céanna uirthi sin chomh maith. Bheir an gearrachaile beag ar láimh a máthar is siúlaíodar siar ciumhais na haille in aonacht. Léim mo chroí. Cheapas siúráilte gurb é an rud ba dheise é a chonac raimh. Thabharfainn mo láimh dheas agus fuil mo dhearna ach bheith amhlaidh, gúna a bheith agam ar aondeantús le gúna mo Mhaim, agus mé bheith ag siúl faobhar na faille siar láimh ar láimh léi. "Féach air sin, a Mhaim, féach air sin, an gúna beag agus an gúna mór in aonacht!" Lig mo Mhaim srann beag míchéatach aisti;— "Í féin a dhein an mheaintínteacht, ní foláir" adúirt sí sar ar iontaigh sí ar a sál isteach abhaile.

Tagann cuirtín dorcha anuas ar an radharc ansan. Blianta fada ina dhiaidh sin do thangás ar bhaicle pháipéirí gearrtha as nuachtáin a mhínigh an scéal uile dom. Conas mar ar bádh Na Lads oíche Shin Seáin Big na bliana dar gcionn. "Local tragedy; 2 drowned in fishing boat" adúirt na cinnlinte. Conas mar a bhí corp amháin faighte is an ceann eile fós gan fáil. De réir a chéile do cheanglaíos le chéile le leideanna, mar ní cuimhin liom riamh éinne ag insint an scéil dom ó bhonn. Conas mar a stop an bád de bharr drochpheitrile is nách raibh aon mhaidí rámha acu. Conas mar a theaicleáil fear m'aintín suas a chapall is cairt is chuaigh isteach 'on Daingean ag triall ar na téadáin faille, ach an fear a bhí ina mbun bhí sé bailithe leis go Sasana, is an eochair don áit a rabhadar cinnithe thíos i dtóin a phóca aige. Conas a d'éirigh an oíche chun starráin, is sa deireadh gur bhris an bád i gcoinne na gcarraigreacha. Na daoine a bhí ag faireadh ar barra na haille ná feacadar faic, bhí sé chomh dubh le pic, ach nuair a fuaireadar bolath na pairifíne ón ineall bhí a fhios acu go raibh an séo suas. Gur léim Séan saor ar an gcloich i dteannta an triú duine a bhí mar pháirtí acu. Fear de mhuintir Shé ó Bhaile na hAbhann na Cúlach Thuaidh a bhí sa bhád leo, agus ba iad a bhróga táirní a shaoir é. Do ghreamaíodar leis an gcloich ar feadh na hoíche é is an fharraige cháiteach ag gabháilt lastuas dó. D'inis sé sin dóibh ina dhiaidh sin gur léim Séan leis slán ar dtúis ach nuair a thuig sé nach raibh aon fháil ar Eoghan go ndúirt sé ná féadfadh sé aghaidh a thabhairt abhaile ar a mháthair gan é is gur léim sé isteach sa bhfar raige arís ag cuardach a dheartháir. D'fhan sé féin ar an gcloich go maidin, is na bróga tairní ag tabhairt greama ar éigean dó. Thairrig sé na bróga tairní céanna go trom ina dhéidh agus é ag tabhairt aghaidh ar an bPaddock, ag déanamh comhbhróin le máthair na beirt deirtheárach. Bhí m'athair istigh sa chistin nuair a tháinig sé. "Is orm a bhí an dochma roimh teacht anseo," adúirt sé i mbéal an dorais. Tar éis dó na focail chuí ará (agus cad iad na focail chuí ina leithéid sin de chás?) chas sé ar a shál ins na bróga tairní chéanna is thug a aghaidh arís ar an mbóthar ó thuaidh is ar an mbaile. Bhailibh sé leis go Meiriceá go geairid ina dhiaidh sin is níor fhill sé riamh ó shin. Nó má fhill féin, is i nganfhios dúinne é.

Ach an uair úd nuair a bhíos beag, ní raibh aon ruainne de seo ar eolas gam. Coimeádadh an t-eolas uainn, ar chúiseanna a bhí creidiúnach go maith ag an am is dócha ach a d'fhág mearbhall síoraí orm i dtaobh na tréimhse sin. Níl a fhí os agam faic ach go rabhas thar n-ais i gCiarraí arís, ar feadh tréimhse fada an uair seo, agus ní sa Phaddock in aon chor a bhíos níos mó ach thall i gCathair a' "Treanntaigh in aonacht lem chol ceathrar, Beití.

Bhíos le bheith ag dul ar scoil in aonacht léi sa bhfómhar agus níorbh aon iontas é sin ann féin, mar bhí sí sin tar éis seal a chaitheamh ag dul ar scoil im' theanntasa thall is Sasana. San am sin shiúlaíodh leanaí na Cathrach siar an míle slí a bhí sa Bhóithrin Dorcha go scoil Chaitlíona Naofa i gCill Mhic a' Domhnaigh. Bhí triúr gearrachaillí beaga le bheith i rang na Naíonán Sinsearach, mise agus Beití, mo chol cheathrar, agus comharsa linn, Nuala Long. Lucht an Chomhairle Chontae, a bhíodh ag obair ar na bóithre, thugaidís na "day-old chicks" orainn, bhí cuma chomh bídeach san orainn. Bhí bliain caite ar scoil ag an mbeirt eile agus mise fós thall i Sasana, agus bhíothars amhrasach fúmsa, an cailín Sasanach, féach an ndéanfainn an bheart, is an méid sin de bhóthar a shiúl gach lá. Cuirfeadh ceann des na cailíní críonna, Joan Shea, siar im theannta lá chun mé a thríáil. Tráthnóna bog ceobhránach i ndeireadh Lúnasa ab ea é, bhí an ceo ina bhrat bán ag teacht anuas go sciortaí Sléibhe an Iolair. Bhí gliogar uisce le clos ar dheis mar a raibh uisce na báistí ag draenáil síos ón gcnoc agus isteach ins na corraithe ag Lúb a' Chaoil. Bhí seordán ós na failltreacha ar chlé ag Cuas Crom ag cur in úil duit go rabhadar ann mar leis an mbrat smúite a bhí ar an lá ní raibh radharc ar bith ar an bhfarraige. Seachas dhá ghlór san na n-uiscí éagsúla ní raibh rud ar bith le clos. Bhí boladh mismíne ag teacht chughainn ós na corraithe agus cumhracht eile cosúil le boladh plumaí ó bhláthanna an aitinn agus ón dtáithfheileann go háirithe sa chuid sin den mbóthar atá ar nós tolláin fada glas mar nách bhfuil de leithead ann ach oiread is a scaoilfeadh capall faoi úmacha tríd toisc gur scaoil na tionóntaithe na clathacha amach ar an dá thaobh le teann díocais agus scaimh chun talún. Shiúlamair linn an míle slí siar go siopa Mhártan, seanduine a chónaigh i dtigín beag a bhí buailte suas in aice na scoile agus d'iarramair leathphíunt pairifíne air i gcómhair an tine "primus". Cheannaíomair luach pingne de mhilseáin ghalúin uaidh. Cúig cinn an phingin a bhíodar seo ach thug Mártan ceann breise dhúinn toisc gurb ón gCathair sinn, agus ón mbaile sin ab ea a mháthair féin. Bhí smut de cheirt casta i mbéal an bhuidéil phairifíne, ag déanamh gnó coirc. Bhí dath corcra ar an bpairifín.

85

Bhí boladh láidir air freisin. Bhí gach aon dath faoin spéir ar na sleimidí is na piastaí eile a bhi le feiscint ina gcéadta feadh na slí, agus iad meallta amach ag an mbáistigh, drúchtáin mhóra mhéithe a bhailítí le tabhairt mar bhia dos na lachain a bhí fiain ina ndiaidh, nó seilmidí go mbímist ag imirt leo, á gcur ag rásaíocht ar an bpábhaille aníos ón nGeata Beag nó á gcrá le cipíní adhmaid;—"Sleimidín sleimidín, cuir amach t'adharca, tá na ba san eorna is béarfaidh siad greim ort."

B'sin ceann des na cluichí a mheileadh an asimsir dúinn ins na tráthnóintí fada samhraidh agus gramaisc uile an bhaile bailithe i dteannta a chéile. Bhí sé míle míle i gcéin ón saol a bhíodh á chleachtadh agamsa go dtí san thall i Sasana, áit a rabhas im' leanbh aonair dúnta isteach i ngairdín mór ag imirt liom féin. Bhí sé seo míle uair níos faarr, ag troid is ag áiteamh is ag seó gan stad le scata leanbh beag eile. Ghlacadar go fonnmhar liom chomh luath is a chasas ar Ghaolainn, cé go mbíodh ceist anois is arís i dtaobh an tsaoil úd thall i Sasana. An raibh aon chairde agam ann? Ní raibh. Bhuel, cén sórt cluichí a bhíodh agam mar sin, gan chairde? Ó, adeirinnse go hárdnósach, ní raibh aon ghá le cluichí mar bhí an Telly againn. Chuireadh san an gobán orthu. Agus cén sórt ainmhí ab ea an Telly, an raibh ceithre cosa faoi, an raibh clúmh is eireaball air? Ó, adeirinnse, agus mo shrón san aer agam, níorbh aon ainmhí é an Telly ach bosca. Níorbh aon nath leo an méid sin, nách raibh boscaí anseo chomh maith, agus ní mór na cluichí a fhéadfá a imirt leo. Sea, adeirinnse, ach níorbh aon bhosca mar iadsan an Telly, a dhuine, ach bosca ar leith, bosca go mbíodh daoine agus tithe agus ainmhithe ann. Stadaidís suas des na seilmidí agus thagadh na ceisteanna chomh tiubh le tiul. Daoine istigh i mbosca, cén sórt daoine? Bhuel, adeirinnse, Hopalong-Cassidy Clippedy-clippedy-clop agus Robin-Hood-Robin-Hood-riding-through-the-glen agus an fear ab fhearr ar fad acu, an Cisco Kid, gaiscíoch caol dorcha ar chapall bán faoina spoir óir agus faoina dhiallait airgid a bhuadh ar na bligeardaithe i gcónaí agus a lamhachach san aer lena phiostal greanta ag rá "He Amigo He Pancho". Bhídist ag éisteacht liom go dtí san ach nuair a chloisidís na focail dheoranta ba leor san, tuigtí doíbh go rabhas ag dul ró fhada ar fad leis mar scéal agus go b'ann a bhíos á dhéanamh suas ó thúis deire, ag scaitseáil éithigh mar ba ghnáth. Scaiptí an draíocht agus leanaimís orainn arís leis na seilmidí;—"Sleimidín, sleimidín, cuir amach t-adharca, tá na ba ag búiríl is cuimleoidh siad a leadhb ort."

Théadh díom glan a chur in úil díobh go raibh an saol "amuigh" deifriúil go maith agus gurb shin an fáth a thógainn ceann chomh mór sin des na rudaí is simplí amuigh, rudaí ná cuimhneoidís féin in aon chor orthu, bhíodar chomh comónta san. Ainmneacha na bhFailltreacha mar shampla, a bhí ina liodán fada focalach, agus draíocht ag roinnt le gach focal acu;—"Cuas na Móiníallach, Leacacha na bhFaoileán, Lic Caoil, Lic a' Chosáin, Cuas an Iarainn, Leac an Chréithir, Cuas an Mhadra, Cuas a' tSioda, Báisín an Ghearaltaigh, Cuas Crom." Agus bhíodh a thuilleadh acu leis ann mar bhí ainm ar gach gort ar an mbaile agus ainm ar gach charraige nó cloch shuaithinseach a bhí ins gach gort; - Port na gCnocán, Gort a'Ghalláin, An Móinéar, An Mún, An Garraí Mór, An Garraí Nua, An Rúiscín. Bhí banríon curtha faoin ngallán mór i ngort an tSíthigh is séard a bhí i Lic Caoil, ná fahtach mór a bhí fadó ann, Caol Mac Criothainn, gur dhein leac mór dó tar éis a bháis. Bhí ainm ar gach bóthar agus smut de bhóthar, ó Bhóthar Rí an Aonaigh a tháinig anuas ó Chuas na Míol, An Bóithrín Dorcha, An Bóithrín Caol, go Bóthar Chéileachair a ghaibh sall thar an Ghullet sa Mheis go Claí an Aitinn agus ansan amach ar an mbóthar mór ar theorainn bhaile fearainn eile, Baile an Chóta. Agus na bailte fearainn féin, ba liosta le háireamh iad. Chuirinn iachall ar mo chol cheathrar suí ar chlaí agus iad a ainmniú amach dom, ó cheann ceann an pharóiste; - Fán, Cill Mhic a' Domhnaigh, Cathair Boilg, Baile an Chóta, Baile an tSléibhe Beag, Baile an tSléibhe Mór, Cill Uraidh, Baile an Liaigh, Com a' Liaigh, Baile Treasna, Rath Fhionnáin, Baile Beag, Láthair Fhraoigh, Mám an Óraigh, Ceanntrá, Imleach Shlat agus ar ais go dtí Fionntrá i lár an pharóiste. Tuigeadh dom go raibh draíocht ag roinnt leo, bhíos mar a bheinn faoi dhraíocht acu. Bhí mar a bheadh sé de gheasaibh droma draíochta orm iad a fhoghlaim agus a chur de ghlanmheabhair agus gach scéal agus píosa eolais a bhaineas leo a thabhairt liom ar ais nó ar éigean. Agus de réir mar a fhásas aníos is mó ná riamh mar chuaigh na geasa doimhne sin i bhfeidhm orm, de réir mar a leathnaigh mo thaithí ar an ndúthaigh amach ó pharóiste Fionntrá gur thóg sé isteach seacht sean-pharóiste na fíor-Ghaeltachta, - sesacht pobail, - agus ansan thairis sin féin anonn thar Mhám Conrach go dtí an Leitriúch — no "laistíos de chnoc", mar a thugann muintir an iarthair air, an áit gurb as dom athair is dá mhuintir le cuimhne na ndaoine. Agus do leathnaigh an tsuim dhiamhair chéanna soir thar Chaisléan Ghriaghaire is ó dheas thar Liospóil agus Abha na Scáil go dtí an Com, mar a bhfuil tigh ag mo dheirtháir faoi scáil Chathair Chon Roí, an dún binne intíre a rianaigh ar chuma sofheicthe agus dodhearmhadta teorainn talúintí an treabhchais, seanthriocha Céad Chorca Dhuibhne. Maireann an áit seo mar chéadghrá is mar athair is máthair in aonacht dom. Gan é táim fós im' dhílleachtaí beag anall ó Shasana, i mo phlanda gan athair gan mháthair. Dá mairfinn céad bliain nó an míle féin, ní éireodh liom teacht go dtína dheireadh, agus fios fátha an aoinscéil ina thaobh a thabhairt liom. Agus is leor liom san. Tá mo bhaile is mo shean-bhuaile agam. Is é tinteán m'anama é agus an laimpín eolais ar mo dhul amú. Is ann atá an tarrac croí, is ann atá an t-ancaire. Agus thairis sin amach leathann soir ó thuaidh uaim is thar bheannaíocha arda Uibhe Ráthaigh ó dheas, an chuid eile de Chontae Chiarraí, atá faraoir, mar Charraig na Siúre an amhráin, thar m-eolas.

# Born in a Market Place

*Bryan MacMahon*

I was four years of age when, taken by the hand, I was led down to our newly built house in Market Street. As the name of the street implies, our back gate now opened onto the marketplace itself; standing on the "keepstone" on which the two parts of the backgate were anchored I peeped out through a bolthole perhaps six inches square and found myself gazing into a new and magical world — the world of the market.

To make it more personal, my grandfather, old Pat MacMahon, was weighmaster and was thus in charge of the place. He must have been a tenacious old man, for, refusing to have soldiers of the empire billeted upon his home, he was deprieved of his licence as a publican and was later fortunate enough to be appointed to the post he then held.

The marketplace branded me for life. It was thronged with country-folk almost every day of the week. When it wasn't a calf market, it was a pig market or a butter market: on Fridays it was the country produce market — perhaps the most exciting day of all.

The cattle fairs were held in the adjoining streets- directly under my bedroom window as well as in the broad Square. On the occasion of the Old or Big Fairs they spilled into the other streets of the town. There were times when I awoke at daybreak to hear the sound of hooves under my window and to realize that a horse fair was in progress. Donkeys, mules and jennets were also bought and sold on these occasions: these provided a plebeian counterpoint to the three-quarter bred horses destined for the hunting field. The amoniac smell of horse droppings and cowdung lingers in the recesses of my nose to this day.

So I became acquainted with all aspects of country life as seen through the glass of the market. The place had marvellous ancillary goods and produce for sale at its gates and archways.

Scollops or thatching withies, eelfry, cockles sold by the fluted pint glass, salmon, beef sold by the yard and hung on a steelyard or "stiller" to be weighed, periwinkles and seagrass.

There were innocent looking churns which looked as if they contained "home" or sour milk for pot-oven baking, but when the cover was removed — this when the whole area was cautiously surveyed — the vessels were seen to be three quarters full of sea trout or, as we called them, "white" trout known in Irish as "liatháin" or grey trout. The net used for killing these fish was called the "Cauteen" and it had a finer mesh than the net used for salmon — indeed it was sometimes slipped inside the main net for the purpose of holding the smaller fish.

As the Friday produce market drew near I was often deputed to purchase the vegetables for the week or month as the case may be. Buying these in bulk was buying at cost and always proved to work out far cheaper than the price obtaining in the shops. My main commission was to buy a sack of potatoes. I was warned to purchase only those that were balls of flour when boiled - and certainly not those which turned out like bars of soap. An error in this regard was reckoned a calamity. I was seven or eight years of age at the time. I thought of a cunning plan to ensure success on every occasion.

I faced the crowded market. The potato sacks with their owners were ranked against the pillars of the Market sheds. I strolled along the file of vendors, my attention focused on the men from the seashore — this because potatoes from the sandy soil with seaweed as its manure were reputed to be far better for eating than those produced on cutaway bog. As I went I picked up spent matches from the ground.

Back at the first pillar I asked the man if I could have a sample spud. The sack was open and a boiled floury potato offered as example of the finished product. Taking a sample from deep in the sack I marked it as No.1 by sticking a single match into it. Second pillar, the sample was marked by two matches and so on down the line until No.10 which looked weird with ten matches sunk deep into its flesh. This concluded my sampling. I slipped in home then and boiled my store of spuds. Ah, No. 6 was a beauty! I went back to the market and bought No.6 sack.

Not bad for a cute Kerry lad of seven!

I must mention the shawls worn by the farmwives and others: as I recall it the mingling of these coloured garments strengthened the impression that, when one was in the market, one was also in a near-Eastern bazaar.

The wives of the "strong" farmers wore capacious biscuit-coloured woollen shawls each with a delightful hem of tassels and ornamental thread-work in various colours. The quality of the garment — its opulence at times - offered a clue as to how many milch cows were on the husband's farm. Acreage offered a misguided measure, for a farm was then adjudged by such sayings as "He has the grass of sixty cows" or "She took in a fortune of £2,000 to that place". There was also an implicit distinction made between arable and bogland; this distinction was clarified when the grazing of a cow was mentioned. "Turbary" or the right to cut turf on certain defined areas of bogland was also an added bonus relied upon at times of sale, purchase or the making of matches.

As boys we treated those glorious shawls with scant if not impious attention. Stationing ourselves in church directly behind a pair of similarly attired matrons we tied the tassels of adjoining shawls together with "black" or firm knots. When the women parted company at the end of Mass and made to move off in different directions in the church aisle their tugging pulled the shawls off each others' heads, so that the cursory attire beneath was in each case exposed to a mercilous public gaze.

There were other shawls in the marketplace. Fishwomen from Tralee who sold cockles from wicker baskets, wrapping them in clutches of newsprint, wore dark chocolate coloured shawls while our own women from the thatched cottages of the town wore plain black shawls. Swopped over backyard walls to attend the earliest Sunday masses the shawls allowed housewives to attend service anonymously and without the trouble of dressing up. A single eye seen in the upper triangle of the shawl often gave a keen observer a clue as the identity of the woman behind this Irish yashmak.

But for me the most attractive shawl of all was the green and black paisley shawl worn by the women from the other side of the Ferry, that is south of the River Feale and west to the Shannon mouth. "Mahera" we called that area. The old saying "Marry a Mahera woman and you marry Mahera" gave some indication of its clannishness. For me this shawl conveyed an impression mingled of faction fighting, (The Cooleens versus the Mulvihills), hurling — (Ballyduff had already won Kerry's one and only All-Ireland Senior Hurling title) lovely loam, a Round Tower, and the net fisherman of the Cashen estuary with their unusual boats called "ganelows" — probably a corruption of gondola.

All this vanished world, as evoked by the green and black shawl, I experience again on visiting a folk and general museum perched high above the Cashen fishing village, a place familiar to the thousands of visitors to Ballybunion during the summer season.

The marketplace was then shot through with the idealism of freedom; balladsingers, each with his swatch of rebel songs, moved through the throngs. (Later, I wrote many of those ballads for my friend the printer.) The muttering about grabbed farms and rural boycotts were backgroud music to the shouting of castclothes men with their marvellous rhetoric and the land-hungry cry of "The land for the people and the road for the bullock." The accessories for the carts were versatile — the creel or rail for bonnavs, turf or turnips, the seat-and-guards for travelling to town or even to Mass, the low box for carrying sand or gravel while the bare cart itself was capable of being loaded with stable manure or a piled array of sacks of various kinds. The vehicles were locally called Scotchcarts as opposed to the "tumbler from up the country" or even the "slide" used in the Dingle area for bringing down turf saved on the mountain flank.

The colour of the carts was a brilliant orange red with the shaft ends tipped with black: each one had the name of its owner and his townland print-painted in black at the point where the right shaft met the body of the vehicle. I came to know of every townland and of almost every family within thirty miles of my town as a result of perusing these inscriptions. I even made a collection of the townland names, querying the former owner as to where it was situated and more importantly still, the meaning of the Irish version of the name.

The butter market was something I was deeply involved in. As my father's health waned he gave up his law office post and took to buying butter for export, working hand in hand with his brother who was a creamery manager. The butter borer used for testing the country butter took my attention. I learned to insert it in the butter pile, spin it full circle, extract it, smell the butter, bite a chunk of it, roll it round in the mouth as if testing wine, uplift one's judicious eyes to the heavens, spit it out at a certain place in the yard and finally offer a grudged grunt of approval of its merits.

If my grandfather reigned over this colourful kingdom I was often his viceroy. This was when the market was quiet and my grandsire and one of his cronies stole off for a pint. I was then left in charge of the place. I directed horseloads onto the weigh-bridge, weighed them, issued a ticket and later deducted the tare or weight of the unladen vehicle. I progressed so far in my avocation that I could look at a sack of potatoes and tell almost to the pound how much it weighed. I was then about nine or ten years of age.

There was always a double line of horse rails of turf just inside the market gate — a point which was a fruitful source of interest to me. Sometimes I'd find a dead hare hanging from the willow fork which kept the creel in place. The hare was for sale, of course, but I'd ask for, and was given, the tail. It was easy to bargain with the turfsellers on a rainy day as our yard was on the market and the seller sold the turf at a reduced price so as to enable him to go home quickly. I came to know at a glance from which of the many bogs of North Kerry any particular creel of turf came and thus could size up its heating qualities at a glance.

There was one particular turfman who got the better of me in repartee. When I countered his asking a certain price for his load by saying "I could buy a few hundred-weights of good English coal for that" he said quietly, "Do you know what Dean Swift said about that?" "I don't remember," I said. "He advised the Irish people to burn everything English except their coal". After that I always called the man Dean Swift and never after bargained with him about the price of his turf.

So there it was, the market place, still vibrant today but now metamorphosed into a major mart. It branded me deeply with its shawls and carts, its boycott horns and faces, it's hurdy-gurdies and dancing ducks (the duck danced on a griddle when a secret switch was thrown and a weak electric shock troubled the bird's lapeens.) Its sire horses parading in male splendour, its busbies and scarlet jackets of the old time recruiting officers, its drum-beats and grace-noted ballads, its trick-of-the-loop and three-card trick practitioners, its black doctor extracting a tooth with his powerful and bloodied fingers, its grinning monkey on the shoulder of the "Pick and Win" merchant, its delf sellers and pretty-pretty budgerigars picking out fortunes for giggling country girls, its market hall where we had magicians and operatic stars, its aromatic mutton pie shops — all these things were mine and are mine in memory to this day.

I wrote two major radio features on the goings-on of the market — one at the instigation of W. R. (Bertie) Rodgers the poet and Ernie O'Malley. It was called "I was Born in a Market Place" and, broadcast by the BBC on what is called Boxing Day. It had an audience of about twenty million listeners.

Strictly speaking, I was born elsewhere in the town but was transferred to the Marketplace at so young an age as made no matter. The other feature written at the request, I think, of Frank McManus of Radio Eireann, was "The Big Fair Day" and its subject matter was drawn from the same reservoir of memory.

But times change. Today when I visit the new addition to a fine supermarket, inevitably in Market Street, I realize as I wait at the check-out counter, that where I am standing was bang in the middle of the kitchen of my old and colourful home.

# Growing Up in a North Kerry Village

*John Coolahan*

## A Sense of Place

The place where we spend the impressionable and formative years of our childhood and youth becomes a significant part of us on our life's journey. We may scatter far and encounter a great variety of places and cultures but for the vast majority of people a special bonding exists between them and the place in which they grew up. Childhood is wide open to the sights, sounds, smells, colours and encounters of the place which nurtures it. The sense of place, of roots, of belonging, is an important dimension of personality and self-identity.

Growing up as a boy in Tarbert in the forties and fifties has left an indelible imprint on my own consciousness. The places, the personalities and the experiences form a reservoir of pleasurable memories. One considers it a privilege to have grown up in such an interesting place, within a community of great cultural richness and caring humanity.

Among places of enchantment were the woods, with their laurel, chestnut and hazelnut groves. Each season brought its own magic to the woods. Building tree houses in the lushness of summer, gathering conkers in the multicoloured autumn, wandering through the scented bluebells and wild garlic in May and collecting holly and ivy in the cold, bare woods at Christmas time, were some of the seasonal variations of activity. Born by the sea, one never loses the sound of the sea and the majestic Shannon estuary at Tarbert was a continual fascination in a whole variety of ways. There was swimming in the favoured spots such as Rusheen, Wall's Bay, the Slatey Pier, the Island and the Back-o-the-hill. There was fishing from the pier and on "The Bank". Periwinkles, bornachs and mussels were in profusion and unpolluted along the shores. The tides came and went in ceaseless motion, ships plied up and down the river, and the curlews, seagulls, swans and widgeon brought the reed-fringed mudflats and creeks to life. Tarbert Island with its lighthouse, battery coastguard station and gantry brought *Treasure Island* and *Coral Island* close to home, and bands of cowboys and Indians, or hordes of cops and robbers worked out their fantastical games in-and-out through the ruins.

In April and May the boglands called for the turf-cutting, and through the summer they spread their splendour of bog-cotton, heathers, furze and many-coloured mosses to enchant the eye. The cutting and saving of hay, with a heavy reliance on manual skill and horse power, had fun as well as work attached to it. The satisfaction of leaving a wyned meadow in the evening sun, with the aroma of freshly saved hay in the nostrils, stays as a haunting memory.

There was no time for boredom, the word was never used. There were many hunts — rabbits, hares, foxes and the occasional badger hunt. The "horse-park" was the mecca for groups of young and established football players in the evenings as aspiring youngsters tried to imitate their heroes. The year was pun-ctuated with a variety of activities and events which were very congenial to youngsters. The great carnivals, which drew huge crowds of all ages to the village, were held in August. The fancy dress parades were highly elaborate and imaginative. It took a couple of hours for all the sections of the parade, from individuals to large groups, to pass through the crowds lining the streets. Horses, tractors and lorries were used by the larger groups for their colourful presentations. Regattas with their boat races, swimming races, greasy poles and pillow fights, brought great excitement to the island. Matches in football tournaments drew large partisan audiences. At night the pubs resounded to laughter, songs, music and arguments. There was no consciousness of a generation gap in the dancers who thronged the marquee. The carnivals may not have had the flamboyance and exhilaration of a mardi gras, but they had as much vitality as an

Irish community could give them. Other summer occasions were marked in different ways, for instance, May Eve was treated with a sense of unease and respect. The summer tree (sycamore) was brought into the houses, and whispers were made of the "piseogs" which could be perpetrated on that evening, which retained vestiges of old pagan folk memory. The old festival of mid-summer was also marked by the mighty bonfires on the Market Road on St. John's night, for which materials were gathered evenings in advance. We danced and played as the flames and sparks went higher in the night sky, giving us feelings, at once, of both fascination and dread.

The autumn evenings were marked by the Listowel races, the All-Ireland final and the Glin Coursing. As altar boys we visited the houses throughout the parish for the stations in the mornings, and attended at the October rosary and benedictions in the evenings. These led on to Halloween, with the excitement of "high-fiddles", snap apple, Halloween games and blind-man's-buff. The abundance of apples, nuts and barmbracks were consumed with relish.

Christmas, of course, was special in the village, as everywhere else. Many of us, however, preferred the activity of Stephen's Day to the quiet atmosphere of Christmas Day. Groups of us gathered and tramped the countryside with the Wren-boys, generally being warmly welcomed and well-treated in the houses which dotted the landscape. Trudging home from the hills of Bally-gaughlin, with lights and Christmas candles lighting the dark, and with many days of Christmas holidays stretching ahead, was a good feeling. New Year's Eve was a special night in the village when crowds gathered in torchlight procession, with accordions and bodhráns bidding farewell to the old year and welcoming the new. The music, dancing and songs carried on in the village square into the early hours.

At other times, the village was entertained by the sounds and smells of the animals, which were part of the agricultural economy of the region. The cattle fairs, bull-tests and pig sales brought varied activity to delight youngsters. The great social occasion of the creamery, particularly on summer mornings, created a buzz of activity and conversation in the village, and also brought town and country close together. The forge with its sizzling fire and sound of the anvil also brought town and country and hedgehogs together, as youngsters vied to blow the large bellows to redden the blacksmith's horseshoes.

The carpenter's shop with its resin-smelling ringlets of shavings was also a place of delights. The whine of the great saws mingled with the carpenter's hammer blows, as cradles, coffins, carts and crates were fashioned. Nearby was the parish hall which housed the billiards club, the hops and the whist drives for the older groups.

The school, for good or ill, is the institution which has a vast range of influences upon us when we are young. Many experiences occured there with life enhancing as well as debilitating effects, but which stay with us to the grave. In our time the tolling of the church bell for mass, angelus, or funeral was close to us in the school. In the church the great events of Catholic life — baptism, confirmation, marriage and funeral — were conducted and, to the eyes of us altar boys, had an interesting ritual about them, if also tinged with trepidation at times. The primary school had been built in 1869 and was strictly segregated between boys and girls. Facilities were rather spartan, and the large rooms depended on the quality of turf, brought by children's parents, for the open fires. Discipline tended to be on the "spare the rod, spoil the child" principle, with catechism class particularly fraught with anxiety. For some of us, practice with the mouthorgan band brightened the rather narrow curricular range, which was based primarily on English, Irish and Arithmetic, with a welcome dimension of History and Geography added.

A minority of pupils went on to secondary school in the nearby St. Ita's. This was one of the small lay, co-educational secondary schools to be found, fairly regularly, in Kerry and Limerick at the time. The founder of the school, Miss McKenna, was a noted educationalist who set high standards as the norm, particularly in her specialist subjects, English and French. She and her team opened up for us teenagers the richnesses of new languages, great literatures, mathematics and so on. It was also an era in which the competition for the public examinations was much less intense than to-day. Pupils cycled and bussed from nearby townlands and villages to the school.

We were always conscious that most parents took schooling seriously, and one took for granted a regard for learning, which was part of the tradition of the region. Both the national and secondary schools bore witness to the long-term impact, which gifted teachers can have, on the attitudes and outlook of youngsters in their formative years. Since that time the "school on the hill" has been replaced by a splendid comprehensive school, and it is gratifying to know that the traditions of good schooling and scholarship are alive and well in that corner of north Kerry.

The forties and fifties were decades of economic depression, and many families suffered from the deprivations of real poverty. Employment, other than in agriculture, was very rare and emigration was the lot of many. It was sad to see many of one's school pals gathering at the corner to catch the bus to Limerick and be on their way to England. To get there, they were often aided by the allowances gained on F.C.A. training camps. It was the scarcity of money which acted as a constraining and blighting force on many people. The fabric of community life was maintained and, often, the very poor did not allow their material impoverishment to quench the spirit of their personalities. To a degree the old proverb "Ar scáth a chéile a mhaireann na daoine" was borne out, and various quiet forms of assistance were available. Nevertheless, life, in general, was affected by the lack of a vibrant economic infrastructure which would provide gainful employment for the people of the area. Even as a youngster, one was conscious of this overlay of economic hard-times, and despite the richness of aspects of community life, the potential of many individuals was not realised.

A striking feature of this community life was the respect for individuals, the tolerance for eccentricities and a regard for the "characters". People were known for particular songs, or yarns, experiences or skills. This I have found to be a strong feature of life in Kerry, but, no doubt, is not inique to it. There is, however, a delight in difference, a pleasure in language usage and a regard for the individual experience, which ia a valuable feature of life there.

## Old Glories Reflected in Stone

Among many features one would like to dwell on, I will touch on one which struck me very forcibly, as a young person, but which was not much mentioned — Tarbert's walls. To a youngster's eye in the forties and fifties there was very little industrial or commercial employment in the village, but all around one were mighty walls and large buildings, many gone into decline and which spoke to one of a different era, a bygone era in a Tarbert which must have been very different. They stood silent as sentinels and witnesses of a Tarbert which must have been more vibrant. They symbolised an era when there must have been great collective endeavour. The question arose as to what had happened in old Tabert that left us so many monuments in stone, which seemed out of keeping with the community's character at the time one was growing up. Only communities with a sense of confidence, of collective purpose and of optimism built on a grand scale, and such optimism was foreign to the decades of the forties and fifties. Another question which arises in one's mind was the number of skilled craftsmen who must have been there to build such splendid edifices. The scale of the building projects would have required a whole sophisticated culture in crafts, but particularly in stone masonry. When I looked at skilled masons in our time, they seemed to be the inheritors of this older tradition. As well as the scale of the buildings and the remaining walls of greater edifices, one was also struck by the beauty of the stone itself and by the skill and sense of pride which exuded from the workmanship.

The surviving evidence went back to the medieval times as evidenced in Kilnaughtin Church and Lislaughtin Abbey. In the latter, the beauty of the dovetailing of the flat river stones with the shaped limestone of sedilia and lintel windows has been beautifully caught by the Polish artist Ursula Ratzlaff O'Carroll. Striking instances from the eighteenth century included Tarbert House, seat of the Leslie family. This early Georgian (1701-1720) country house is a distinctive feature of Ireland's architectural heritage. From the late eighteenth century there was the massive and magnificent Battery perched on the hill of the "old" Tarbert Island. Its huge, cut-limestone blocks and mighty walls seemed to be built for a permanence like the great Temples of the Nile Valley. It was a cause of wonder to us how the blocks were shaped and hoisted to form such a fortress, which was also proportionally a pleasing architectural whole.

However, it was the nineteenth century, and particularly the 1830s and 1840s, which saw the golden age of Tarbert building. Staying on the Island, the graceful edifice of the Tarbert Light-house was built in the 1830s to adorn the Shannon Estuary and give illumination to its sailors. The causeway to the mainland, with its sloping sides, mounted with cut-limestone, was engin-eered and built in the 1830s. Great skill was also evidenced in the "Old" and "New" Piers which were busy ports of call in the nineteenth and early twentieth centuries. It is gratifying to note that the old pier, which has succumbed to the depredations of storms and strong waves, is being restored. Another monument of stone on this nineteenth century island was the large coast-guard station. Part of it was still inhabited in our childhood, but, in the main, it was a gaunt reminder of other days and other rulers, as one rounded the "Black Point," on the island road.

Close to the village on the island road were the still high walls of the great stores built by James Pattison in the 1830s. These stones covered a wide area and had a small landing berth behind the stores which allowed access to craft with commodities, at certain stages of the tide. The store was later owned by the Speight family of Limerick. The lore was still alive in our child-hood of the drowning of a cargo of pigs down the creek from the landing pier. Part of the stores was used as Hill's Creamery at the turn of the twentieth century. The great walls and landing berth still stand but the hustle and bustle of commercial activity is long gone.

A little further on was the splended building of the Bridewell, dating from 1831, that great era of building, the 1830s. It served as a courthouse and jailhouse for several generatons. Some significant trials took place there and, no doubt, the spirit was low of many who entered it's precincts and its cells. In our time it was inhabited by the Burke family, but, as we went in and out through it we often played the role of guards and prisoners. Maurice Craig, the distinguished historian of Irish architecture, has spoken favourably of its design. The stone work was splendid, and great care was exhibited in the window ledges and chimneys, while the great limestone block over the gateway had the single word "Bridewell" engraved, reflective of the power of a particular law system of that era. It is gratifying to see this fine building restored by modern craftsmanship in the last few years, be-tokening a living tradition in stone craft.

Perhaps the greatest building of all was Russell's Store which dominated the lower part of the village. The ground area covered by the store was huge and it soared six storeys over a basement. The great branching stone over the arch lies in the yard today with the words "Russell's Store, 1848" engraved, reminiscent of Ozymandias's monument lying low on the desert sands of Egypt —proclaiming a former era of power and confidence. That this massive building was erected in famine times, in 1848, tells of much activity and a cohort of skilled craftsmen in gainful employ-ment in those harrowing years. The upper storeys were knocked in the 1940s, leaving the surrounding walls still there as reminders of a more commercial past. Kelly's butcher's shop of today keeps a commercial presence on the site.

Up the market road was the great Market Field, again surrounded by well-built walls and entered through impressive gateways, with cut-stone stiles on each side. The market field and the adjacent walled pound field used by us for playing, with occasional visits of circuses and carnivals, brought home to us the reflection of an older, commercial community, and the ivy clad walls told their own story.

The extraordinary building activity of the 1830s and 1840s is again driven home as we note the building of the Parish Hall in 1831, which served as Tarbert's first national school in 1836, following the establishment of the new national school system in 1831. Daniel O'Connell, a regular visitor to Tarbert in those years, led the Catholic Emancipation campaign to victory in 1829. Shortly after, Fr. McCarthy built St. Mary's Catholic Church, off the new Mail Road to Listowel, in 1833. This beautiful old church was renovated by Tarbert craftsmen in the mid 1950s. Tarbert's purpose-built national school was designed to Board of Works specifications, in 1869. It, again, was a triumph of the stonemason's craft and was a fine specimen of the traditional national school. As school children we had a good reason to note all the details of stone craft, with windows, doorways, chimneys, embellishing the structure. Another splendid specimen of stone building was the parochial house. The Tarbert community kept faith with that impressive tradition of stone-building by ensuring that the building was refurbished a few years ago, in such a way that its external beauty of stone design will be a heritage for future generations.

The shaping of Tarbert Square was also, mainly, a development of the 1830s, following the improved road network of the 1820s. The largest buildings surrounding the impressive Square were those we knew as the "Hotel" and the "Post Office". These were very impressive stone buildings and the mighty walls towered high. Both were still inhabited in the 1940s but, as time evolved, they again became further reminders of a bygone age, when Tarbert had five hotels and the Bianconi cars delivered their passengers and commodities to the Square.

The great walls of the hotel compound went down the Glin Road and encompassed other houses, since gone. Opposite, on Artillery Parade, were, again, impressive houses, now occupied by the Lavery and Murphy families. As children we liked to gather outside the old Wesleyan Church on the Glin Road,

103

particularly at Harvest Thanksgiving, to hear our fellow parishioners honour God within their rites. The plain stone building reflected the diverse character of the denominations, and was surrounded with a quiet aura of dignity. The fine stone building on the hill, the old eighteenth century Erasmus Smith School was now St. Ita's College, with a lovely stone Protestant national school alongside.

A little bit further on was another jewel of the stone mason's craft, the Church of Ireland house of worship, with its four spires a landmark in the landscape. It too spoke to us of another era, coming down to us from 1814.

Monuments in stone are a physical reminder of locations and buildings which surrounded one in growing up. Many of the other memories have a less tangible reflection, but become imprinted on one's consciousness in subtle ways and blend into memory's kaleidoscope.

The places, the seasons, the events, the personalities, all helped to form a rich tapestry of experience. Here one has been etching in some of the main threads, but a multiplicity of minor threads enmeshed with these to form a whole. Within that whole, place, community, tradition, personality, story, song, music, dance, legend, imagination criss-crossed in the weave and helped to fashion us as people, inheritors of much humanity and enabled us to contribute to its further enrichment.

# A Kerry Suite

*Gabriel Fitzmaurice*

## 1. Hence the Songs

i.m. Billy Cunninghan, singer

How soon great deeds are abstract...

Hence the songs—
The mighty deeds the tribe sings in the bar:
*Gaisce* diminished by the video.

Men I never knew still star
In North Kerry Finals,
Their deeds not history but myth
Alive upon a singer's breath;

Again local men are martyred
In a lonely glen;

Now love is lost,
A Rose is won -

Things insufficient till they're sung.

## 2. Lovers

Is it the clothes
Or is it the socks?
There's a sweet smell of dirt off me.
I smell of my friends
— Must take a wash.

A lunatic laughs at Mass.
(It's really a sin,
But to be normal
Is to laugh at him.)

He laughs at us:
At our cleanliness,
At our fuss.
Better to go and hustle
Like him.

Your car was wrecked,
You buy one new.
Who hasn't a ha'penny
Well God bless you.

The river, convulsed
Like a lunatic
Stormed on a table,
Is called Annamoy.
I love it
Because it's a hopeless river.
But sun, clouds, cows
Quiver in it;
Wagtails ripple over it
While bulls trample its stones.

The village is Newtown Sandes
(Called Moyvane
—The Middle Plain —
For hate of landlords.)
New people don't like it:
It's like haze on a hill.

I want to die in it.

Like the mad
Flirting with the happy and sad
And hope and the rope
And water,
The people like islanders
Await the disaster
And live.
Dogs and simpletons
Plough the midday swirl of dust
And papers.

I did a line with the city,
Made love to a town,
But always that dung-sotted river
Leafed me home.

Newtown you bastard
You'll break me I know;
New women won't live here,
Our women have left here,
And always I grow old.
Like a dog and its master,
Like a ship on the water,
I need you, you bitch,
Newtown.

I need you, you bitch,
Newtown.

### 3. Derelicts

Whenever I picture the village fools
They drool with the hump
Of benevolence on their backs.
Living in hovels as I remember
They had the health of the rat.

They perched on the street-corner
Like crows around the carcass
Of a lamb. Stale bread and sausages
Would feed a hungry man.
Beady with the cunning of survival
Each pecked the other from his carrion.

Children feared them like rats in a sewer:
They stoned their cabins
And the stones lay at the door.

Like priests, they were the expected,
The necessary contrary —
We bow in gratitude for mediocre lives;

We keep the crow, the rat from the garden.
Like priests, no one mourned when they died.

When they died, we pulled down their cabins.
Then we transported a lawn
That the mad, the hopeless might be buried
— Only the strong resisting while strong;
We kept the grass and flowerbeds neatly
But the wilderness wouldn't be put down.

Children no longer play there
(They stone it),
Nettles stalk the wild grass,
Scutch binds the stones together...

Then came the rats.

### 4. Hay
   for my father

**I**

Heavy bales are hoors.
The shed is no place
If you're not too strong.
Sweat sticks
Like hay to wool
And the rhythm of hay
Is the last native dance.
Will it ever stop,
This suicidal monotone of hay?
It goes on like a depression
In the rural brain.

**Hay**
(Long ago the days were longer)

**Hay**
(Long ago the men were stronger)

**Hay**
(Long ago you gave a day's labour

For a day's pay)
(It didn't rain in summer long ago)

**Hay Hay Hay**

**II**

I bought a bulk milk container,
I built another shed,
Everyone advised me that
The ass-and-cart, the tank
Were dead.

My father would surely wonder now
At the size of my great herd.

I've bulldozed uneconomic ditches
That made *Garraí Beag, Fearann, Móinéar—*
This great new field I'm fencing
Has no name.

My father
Spoke to his cows in winter
In the stall.
Connor knew his herd by name;
He fed them on the *long acre*
And was put in jail.

There was a priest here once
Who ranted that a man
Measured his importance
In the size of his dung-hill,
The poor clout!

Nowadays
You measure your importance
In the size of your bulk container.
Shortly they'll open
"The Club of the Bulk Container:
Farmers not allowed."

The good is modern -
You can't opt out.

**III**

Once I made wynds
In small meadows for fear of rain.
Some of the hay was green.
A friendly dog kept jumping on my back.
We had time for a fag
And porter at the gap.

Later
We milked the cows by hand
And strained the milk with a rag —
"A white cloth", we called it.
We laughed in those days

We did
We did

We laughed...

**5. A Game of Forty-One**

Tonight it's forty-one;
Pay to your right, 10p a man.
Doubles a jink, and play your hand.
If you renege, we'll turn you.

Yes, tonight it's forty-one:
A table for six, any pub in town.
Follow suit, and stand your round.
If you renege, we'll turn you.

Tonight it's forty-one
And tomorrow in the Dáil
Fine Gael and Fianna Fáil
Debate their Bill —

Cos on the television
They're talking of revision

And extension of detention
And extra Special Powers.

So we sit here hour by hour
Getting drunk on special Power:
A game of cards at night now
Costs more and more and more.

And you trump hard on the table,
And you pay up when you're able.
If you don't, then you're in trouble
— It's worse than to renege.

Oh, it's always forty-one:
Play your cards at work, at home —
Even sitting on a barstool
They won't let you alone.

Yes, it's always forty-one,
And I'm really in the dumps
For the horsemouth at my elbow
Has just led the Ace of Trumps.

And I'm playing forty-one
And wishing there were some
Other way of spending
A lifetime in this town.

But the poet and the priest
— Beauty and the Beast —
Must all sit down together
And cut this common deck.

And there is no Bill or Bible
But the verdict of the table
And the argument of players
To dispute the point of rule.

So tonight it's forty-one
And tomorrow, next week, next month,
And I'm out if I suggest
Another rule.

## 6. Virgin Rock, Ballybunion

for Johnny Coolahan

Surrounded by breakers,
I stand
Where the grinding ocean
Turns weakness into sand.
I approach my true shape,
Being weathered —
Cliff to rock to strand...

## 7. Dancing Through

Homage to Mikey Sheehy, footballer

Nureyev with a football,
You solo to the goal
Where the swell of expectation
Spurts in vain —
O master of the ritual,
O flesh of tribal soul,
Let beauty be at last
Released from pain...

Now grace eludes its marker
Creating its own space
While grim defenders
Flounder in its wake;
And the ball you won from conflict
Yields to your embrace —
Goal beckons like a promise...
And you take.

## 8. Galvin and Vicars

i.m. Mick Galvin, killed in action, Kilmorna, Knockanure (in the parish of
Newtown Sandes, now Moyvane) on Thursday, 7 April, 1921; Sir Arthur
Vicars, shot at Kilmorna House, his residence, on Thursday, 14 April, 1921.

Mick Galvin, Republican,
Arthur Vicars, who knows what? —
Some sort of loyalist,

In Ireland's name were shot —

Vicars by Republicans,
Galvin by the *Tans,*
Both part of my history -
The parish of Newtown Sandes

Named to flatter landlords
(But "Moyvane" today,
Though some still call it "Newtown":
Some things don't go away

Easily.) Galvin and Vicars,
I imagine you as one —
Obverse and reverse
Sundered by the gun.

History demands
We admit each other's wrongs:
Galvin and Vicars,
Joined only in this song,

Nonetheless I join you
In the freedom of this state
For art discovers symmetries
Where politics must wait.

**9. Saint Stephen's Day**

Poverty reduces fathers
To begging on the Wren...
This battered old Cortina
Is driven by a man

Forced to exploit his family —
His four face-blackened sons
Split up to beg from door to door.
This kind of Wren's no fun,

This single plea for charity
At every private door—

Some will give a good heart,
Some say the time's too poor

For Wren Boys.
Today in Brosnan's Bar
This father came in shyly,
He'd no money for a jar;

He sang a verse of *Spancil Hill*,
The tremor in his voice
Was fear — fear of tomorrow.
It was the voice of Christ

Tugging at my conscience
And at my overdraft,
At the candle in my window:
"Put Christmas in his cap".

Every coin I paid him
Was one that I could spare -
What's a few pints less at Christmas
And half the country poor?

But every coin contributed
Indicts the status quo
Of forcing fathers on the Wren
Blacking-up their woe.

## 10. Saint Stephen's Night in Kearney's Bar, Moyvane

In Kearney's time is music
As Wren Boys take a break
Fabulously mortal;
Here for a while they play —

Brendan Moloney and Dan Connor
Costumed for this night,
Wren Boys bringing Christmas
(Given sup and bite

By neighbours for whom Christmas
Would be poor and mean

Without the hope of pageant).
A dozen tambourines

Fall silent as the couple
Draws elated whoops
From the careless heart of company —
A pair of souls who swoop,

Protected by their music,
To the dying of the light
To emerge again triumphant
Then go into the night

Leaving here behind them
In this sanctuary of sound
A turf-fire of good spirits
As the New Year comes around.

## 11. New Year's Eve
### for Brenda

It's New year in the village,
The torches dance and flare
At midnight, and still no-one
Seems to know they're there.

Too many years unnoticed,
Too much private cheer
Have left our youth ignorant
Of ringing-in the year.

In a covenant of porter
This ceremony was planned,
And tonight the parish Wren Boys
Have gathered in a band

To defy the death of custom;
Their torches dance and flare —
The only time that's lost to us
Is when we're not aware.

Banjo, flute, accordion,
Mandolin and drum
Play us through the village.
From every pub they come

Through the open doors of midnight
Those tacit 'afterhours'
That don't exist officially);
The blazing torches shower

Sparks that shoot and sizzle
Like static in the night
Then disappear forever
Into the hidden sight

That animates the darkness
And shapes this wild parade —
Rituals of midnight
That wake up half dismayed...

## 12. Port an bPúcaí

 for Tony Mac Mahon


"Music of the Fairies" —
I wonder what he knew:
He heard a world and named it;
Came back to tell it, too.
Possessed by so-called "fairies",
The fiddler had to find
A beauty that would please him
As they played upon his mind.

"Music of the Fairies"—
Like any poet he knew
That beauty would destroy him
Unless he made it, too...

## 13. Footballers

 Homage to Jack O'Shea, footballer

We live with the possibility of Gods
As men fulfil their manhood in the fray;
All is truth, we're everything that happens —
We see ourselves reflected in the play.

As Dads line out with sons in local matches
To fill a team whose youth have gone away,
They shoulder hope, taking on our sorrows
When they tog out in our colours and are gay.

So thank you, then, for showing that the spirit
Is a ball that's fielded, worked upon the ground;
Gods are men who suffer to inspire us...
I've watched the game, and this is what I've found.

### *Notes*

**Hence the Songs:** *Gaisce* is Irish for valour, great exploits,
boasting.

**HAY:**   *Garraí Beag:* The Small Garden
        *Fearann:* A Field, Ploughland
        *Móinéar:* A Meadow
        *The Long Acre:* The grass margin at the side of the road

**A Game of Forty-One:** *We'll turn you* means we'll put you out
of this play, this round of cards.

### Port na bPúcaí:

"The Fairies' Music", a Blasket Island air. It was believed to
have been heard from the fairies and translated to the fiddle by
a Blasket fiddler. It has been suggested that the air is based on
the call of a seal (or a whale) heard at night on *Inis Icíleáin,* the
most southerly of the Blaskets.

117

# Biographical Notes

**Paddy Bushe** was born in Dublin in 1948 and was educated at U.C.D. Until 1991 he taught in Waterville where he still lives. A poet, he has published Poems With Amergin ( Beaver Row press, Dublin 1989), Teanga (Coisceim, Dublin 1990) and Counsellor (Sceilg press 1991).

**John Coolahan** was born in Tarbert in 1941 and received his early education in the local National School and at Saint Ita's Col lege, Tarbert. Professor of Education at Saint Patrick's College, Maynooth, he has taught also at primary and post-primary levels. He has lectured and published extensively at home and abroad. His books are Irish Education: Its History and Structure (Institute of Public Administration, Dublin 1981) and The A.S.T.I. and Post Primary Education in Ireland 1909-1984 Cumann na Meáanmhúin teoirí, Éire, Dublin 1984).

**Mary Cummins** is a journalist with The Irish Times.

**Gabriel Fitzmaurice** was born in 1952 in Moyvane in North Kerry where he lives and teaches in the local National School. Poet, translator and editor he has published some fifteen books among them The Father's Part (Story Line Press, Oregon 1992), The Space Between: New and Selected Poems 1984-1992 (Clo Iar Chonnachta, Conamara 1993), Nocht (Coiscéim, Dublin 1989), The Moving Stair (Children's verse - Poolbeg, Dublin 1993), The Flowering Tree/An Crann Faoi Bhlath (contemporary poetry in Irish with verse translations - Wolfhound Pres, Dublin 1991) and Irish Poetry Now - Other Voices (Wolfhound Press 1993).

**John B. Keane**, born in Listowel in 1928, is one of Ireland's most popular authors and a major Irish playwright. His latest book is The Contractors (Mercier Press 1993), a novel. He has written many bestsellers including the novels The Bodhrán Makers (Bran don 1986) and Durango (Mercier 1992) and plays The Chastitute and The Field — now a major film. He lives in Listowel where he presides over his renowned hostelry.

**Brendan Kennelly**, one of Ireland's most popular poets, was born in Ballylongford in North Kerry in 1936. He has published over 20 books of poetry including The Book of Judas (Bloodaxe 1991) which topped the Irish bestsellers list. He is professor of Modern Literature at Trinity College, Dublin.

**Mick MacConnell** was born in 1947 in Enniskillen Co. Fermanagh. Having left school early, he came to journalist after working in a variety of jobs. He was a journalist in the Irish Press Group and in The Irish Times, and is presently a columnist with The Kerryman. One of Ireland's leading songwriters, his first album Peter Pan and Me was an outstanding critical and popular success. He lives in Listowel with his wife and family.

**Steve MacDonogh** was born in Dublin in 1949 and educated in England. Since 1982 he has lived in Dingle where he is editorial Director and co-founder of Brandon, the book publisers. A poet, his latest collection is By Dingle Bay and Blasket Sound (Brandon 1991).

**Bryan MacMahon**, born in Listowel in 1908, is one of Ireland's greatest and best-loved writers. By profession a National Teacher, he is a short story writer, novelist, playwright, storyteller, children's author and writer of ballads and pageants. His latest book, The Master (Poolbeg 1992), memoirs of his teaching days, headed the Irish bestsellers lists. He still lives in Listowel, bailó Dhia air!

**Clairr O'Connor** was born in Limerick in 1951. Educated at Saint Mary's Convent, Limerick. U.C.C. and Saint Patrick's College, Maynooth, she has published a volume of poetry, When You Need Them (The Salmon, Galway 1899) and a novel, Belonging (Attic Press, Dublin 1991). She lives in Maynooth.

**Lily Van Oost** was born in Antwerp in Flanders and now lives and works as a visual artist in the Black Valley near Killarney. She is an Irish citizen. She has been writing all her life and has written poetry, a libretto for an opera, an autobiography and a diary. A book of her drawings, Cyclonic Depression, has been published in Antwerp by Mercator Press. Her Facelift installation on the Ha'penny Bridge for Dublin, capital of culture attracted much notice.

**Nuala Ní Dhomhnaill** was born in Lancashire in 1952 and grew up in the Dingle Gaeltacht in Nenagh, Co. Tipperary. She studied at U.C.C. where she was to return as writer-in-residence. She lives in Dublin with her Turkish husband and four children. Perhaps the most celebrated poet writing in Irish she has published a number of collections including An Dealg Droighin (Mercier 1981), Féar Suaithinseach (An Sagart 1984), Feis (An Sagart 1991) and The Astrakhan Cloak (with translations into English by Paul Muldoon, Gallery Books 1992).